POE *for Your*
PROBLEMS

POE *for Your* PROBLEMS

Uncommon Advice from History's *Least* Likely Self-Help Guru

Catherine Baab-Muguira

RUNNING PRESS
PHILADELPHIA

Running Press
Hachette Book Group
1290 Avenue of the Americas, New York, NY 10104
www.runningpress.com
@Running_Press

Printed in the United States of America

First Edition: September 2021

Published by Running Press, an imprint of Perseus Books, LLC, a subsidiary of
Hachette Book Group, Inc. The Running Press name and logo is a trademark
of the Hachette Book Group.

The Hachette Speakers Bureau provides a wide range of authors for speaking
events. To find out more, go to www.hachettespeakersbureau.com or call
(866) 376-6591.

The publisher is not responsible for websites (or their content) that are not
owned by the publisher.

Print book cover and interior design by Rachel Peckman.

Library of Congress Control Number: 2021009887

ISBNs: 978-0-7624-9909-0 (hardcover), 978-0-7624-9908-3 (ebook)

LSC-C

Printing 1, 2021

There are some secrets that do not permit themselves to be told. Men die nightly in their beds, wringing the hands of ghostly confessors, and looking them piteously in the eyes—die with despair of heart and convulsion of throat, on account of the hideousness of mysteries which will not *suffer themselves* to be revealed.

EDGAR ALLAN POE
1840

CONTENTS

Introduction: The Power of Poe-sitive Thinking.. ix

Before You Move On: Poe's Most Important Poe Tip for You, Plus a Word
  about the French, Who Got Here First.. xvii

Part 1: Starting Out

Lesson #1: Lose Early, Lose Often 2

Lesson #2: Embracing Your Inner Neurotic.. 10

Lesson #3: Hubris, or How to Begin Your Life's Work 18

Lesson #4: Chip on Your Shoulder? Good!..25

Lesson #5: Dealing with Rejection (and Vowing Your Revenge)........33

Part 2: Career and Poe-sonal Finance

Lesson #6: Why Selling Out Is Your First Step to Success....................44

Lesson #7: Fast-Talking Your Way into a "Real" Job..............................53

Lesson #8: What Color Is Your Seashell Scam? 61

Lesson #9: How to Conduct Yourself in a Feud 70

Lesson #10: Sneaking into the C-Suite 79

Part 3: Sex and Death

Lesson #11: How to Lose at Love like a Real Romantic 90

Lesson #12: Pathological Mate Selection..99

Lesson #13: Poe-creation.. 107

Contents

Lesson #14: Sliding into Their DMs (and Other Disasters) 116
Lesson #15: Galaxy Brain, or Making the Most of
        Your Nervous Breakdown 124

Part 4: Making Art and Enemies

Lesson #16: How the Creative Sausage Gets Made........................... 136
Lesson #17: Thriving Through Self-Sabotage 145
Lesson #18: Trolling as a Fine Art.. 154
Lesson #19: Congrats! Attracting Haters Means You Have Arrived 162
Lesson #20: Composing Your World-Changing Masterpiece............. 170

Part 5: The Poe-pose Driven Life: Advanced Techniques

Lesson #21: Personal Growth via Awful, Shocking Vices 182
Lesson #22: Why You Must Question "Reality" 191
Lesson #23: The Case for Relentless Pessimism................................... 199
Lesson #24: Achieving Immortal Renown Through Bad Behavior 207

Addendum: Twenty-Five Ways to Roast a Raven 217
Coda: Poe Won by Losing and You Can, Too 222
Final Quiz: How Poe Are You? 230
Acknowledgments 232
References 233
About the Author.. 234

INTRODUCTION

The Power of Poe-sitive Thinking

If comedy is tragedy plus time, then Edgar Allan Poe's life reads like a punchline—just one long, sad trombone.

Here's the short, oversimplified version: Everyone got sick and everyone died, starting with both Poe's parents before he turned three. A wealthy family adopted him, but only in an informal sense. He lived with them, but he never really belonged, and about the time he reached eighteen, Poe found himself penniless and disowned, forced to craft his masterpieces in cold, dirty, rented rooms.

Later, his beloved wife, Virginia, contracted the same disease that had killed his biological parents, and he became, at last—by his own account—"insane, with long intervals of horrible sanity." Every hand that fed him, he chomped. Every bridge he could burn, he torched. Finally, in October 1849, Poe collapsed in the street outside a tavern, and his career of provocation and troublemaking ground to a halt. In a literal gutter. Yet what followed was even *worse*.

Poe's greatest frenemy, Rufus W. Griswold, wrote his obituary. Publishing his insults under a pseudonym, Griswold told the world that Poe was a cynical, depraved drunk, with no friends, who had only ever used his talent for spite.

The twist? That hit job of an obit turned out to be pretty good PR. Not only did Poe's colleagues and (in fact, numerous) friends sprint to his defense, the notoriety that the obit helped create caused a scandal-loving public to seek out his work as never before. You could say that, in the end, Poe's feuds, mistakes, and missteps worked out for him. Or you could say they weren't mistakes or missteps at all—instead a series of brilliant career moves and an astoundingly effective system for success. Anyone can get to the top doing all the right things. To make it to the top doing all the *wrong* things? Now that takes genius.

Today, nearly two hundred years since his death, millions of people across the globe know and love Poe. He's recognized as one of the most brilliant, original, and influential writers of all time. His poetry and short stories have been translated into every major language and adapted for every new technology, from radio broadcasts to web series to memes. The film and TV adaptations alone—not to mention the references everywhere from *The Simpsons* to *South Park* to Jordan Peele's *Us*—are so numerous it would take ten pages to list them all. He has an awfully long IMDB profile for someone born in 1809.

Poe's fans have included highbrow elites like Vladimir Nabokov and Alfred Hitchcock, and he's enjoyed off-the-charts pop success, too. Baltimore named its NFL team the Ravens. Lou Reed, Joan Baez, and Stevie Nicks have all either recorded songs about Poe or put his words to music. The Beatles stuck him in the top row, eighth from the left, on the cover of *Sgt. Pepper's Lonely Hearts Club Band*. In 2001, Britney Spears kicked off her Dream Within a Dream Tour, while actress Evan Rachel Wood has the final two lines of that poem inked in black across her upper back. As we speak, Sylvester Stallone is trying to produce a Poe biopic. (Hey, Sly, maybe combine it with *Rambo 6*?)

And if you should feel like raising a toast—well, in 2015, Maryland's RavenBeer rolled out Annabel Lee White, "a wheat beer angels envy," and in 2018, a Philadelphia distillery launched a whiskey called Fortunato's Fate. Who wouldn't want to achieve such high-proof prominence, putting so many others under their influence? We should all be so lucky.

Yet somehow the notoriety lingers. Despite Poe's unparalleled worldwide renown, we continue to conceive of him as a ne'er-do-well—just some hopeless, almost Chaplin-esque loser—when the question we should be asking is, "What's his secret?" In a better world, Poe would be considered a self-help guru on par with Oprah, Deepak Chopra, the *4-Hour Workweek* guy, Gwyneth Paltrow, or Dr. Laura Schlesinger. As it is, we celebrate the work but sadly underrate the man.

Except we're not making a mistake about just one man. We're making a mistake about renegades, rebels, and outcasts more generally. We're also making a *very* big mistake in being so certain that we know which creative, professional, and even existential strategies work—and which ones are dead ends. Success on Poe's scale doesn't just happen. It isn't solely a matter of genius, either. It requires a unique vision, and more than that, the fortitude, the determination, the narcissism, and the megalomania to hew to that vision no matter what anyone else says.

It is true Poe's life was a dumpster fire. That's precisely the point. He dealt with horrendous circumstances. He had amply justifiable mental-health issues as well as an impossible personality, and he lived in an absurdly depressing era full of racism, sexism, classism, injustice, misfortune, poverty, disease, and death. You and I live in such an era, too. In a screwed-up world, why not look to the most screwed-up writer of all time for advice on navigating the daily dumpster fires of our own lives? Who better to inspire us as we struggle through our own absurdly depressing time?

Personally, I love nothing more than when a misanthropic supposed "loser" is later wildly, *spectacularly* vindicated. It is like hearing that your own life—no matter this foreclosure you're facing, or the musty Uber you're driving right now—might also end in the best-case scenario. And no one could be more qualified than Poe when it comes to teaching us how to fight through our suffering, how to keep hustling in the face of despair, and how to apologize for getting too drunk (all while ordering "another round for the house, on me!"). In short, how to take the crapola we've been handed and spin it into gold, like Poe did.

So—just how did Poe fail, flail, flub, and flounder his way into the history books? What perverse formula for success can he offer you, and how might you approach your problems a little differently, following his example? That's what you'll find in these pages. Let's seize the day. Or, since we're talking Poe here, seize the night. *Carpe noctem.*

Reading Edgar Allan Poe and parsing his life for instruction might at first seem like a ridiculous exercise, like going fishing in the pool at the Y, or digging for treasure with one of those Allen wrenches you get free from Ikea. And I'll admit this book started as a dark joke—though I'm convinced that's a strength and not a weakness, very much in keeping with Poe's own morbid sense of humor.

A couple of years ago, I was telling a friend how reading Poe's work and the numerous biographies about his life had had the strange effect of helping me cope with the worst depressive episode I've ever experienced, reassuring me that life is worth living at a moment when I was on the verge of ordering a Peloton, and giving me new energy for my creative work. Giving me, of all things, *hope.*

"That sounds like a book," my friend said, lifting his glass.

"Oh yeah," I deadpanned. "I'm going to write a book about reading Poe for self-help and call it *How to Say Nevermore to Your Problems.*" Which turned out to be just the working title.

The point is, Poe can change your life, too. You want to achieve your childhood dreams? You want to humiliate those who've doubted you with your meteoric rise to the top of whatever? All you need is a new perspective—call it Poe-sitive thinking—and that all-important antihero to guide you on your way, helping you discover how to triumph not only in spite of but *because of* your alleged shortcomings. This is where Poe comes in, and how he can illuminate a new path for you as surely as a black light in a sleazy motel room.

Forget everything you've ever assumed about Edgar Allan Poe. Far from being solely a sad story, Poe's own life turns out to be an inspirational tale for black sheep everywhere, so epic and timeless it damn near rises to the level of myth. He might have kicked it seventeen decades ago, yet he's never been more relevant. In fact, his life experience reads like a millennial and Gen Z laundry list. Just for starters, Poe:

- Came of age amidst a dire recession
- Had to drop out of college with mounting debts (150 years before Sallie Mae even existed)
- Got hired, fired, and laid off from a series of journalism jobs at a time of, *ahem*, profound change in the industry
- Was forced to freelance in a burgeoning gig "economy"
- Could barely afford to buy himself a couch, much less a house
- Had no health insurance (couldn't get that dental crown he needed)
- And lived in an America so extremely divided that even the dimmest observers could catch the whiff of impending civil war.

But this book isn't just for young people, or for dedicated Poe fans. This book is for all the hopeless freaks and misfits out there—like you, like me—whose adult lives aren't working out *quite* as we hoped—which we're looking to turn around, somehow. Its whole purpose is to help you find new energy and inspiration so you can follow through on your deepest ambitions despite, well, everything. Your inbox full of rejection letters? Your ex and that restraining order? Forget about 'em. Nevermore, problems!

Let's face it: You've already tried everything else, except the wrong way. The *Poe* way.

Like Poe himself, Poe-sitive thinking is about not just recognizing the dark side of life, but maniacally focusing on it; embracing your over-whelming sense of doom; clinging to your grief; and refusing to give up your most basic resentments. In short, not getting over anything, *ever*, but using all your darkest emotions in novel and creative ways to make a name for yourself and carve out your own unique, notorious place in the world. Let's take a look:

POSITIVE THINKING	POE-SITIVE THINKING
Letting go	Holding on (to grudges, resentments, vendettas, etc.)
Fitting in	Being a unique, utterly one-of-a-kind freak
Having healthy boundaries	Having seething lifelong obsessions
Being happy	Huh?
Making new friends	Smiting thine enemies
Climbing the corporate ladder	Borrowing money from people who climbed the corporate ladder
Wondering if you're doing everything wrong	Wondering if you're doing everything wrong *enough*

If you're heartbroken, lonely, lost, depressed, broke, anxious, under-employed or unemployed, and *especially* if you've recently blown up your life somehow, then congratulations, you've come to the right place. Poe messed up his life again and again, too, only to become more and more successful, and more broadly and intensely beloved. This book will offer you a step-by-step Poe-gram for emulating the man and gleaning all the most important "Poe tips" from his most turbulent life. And because each lesson builds toward the next (complete with exercises, charts, and checklists), I suggest reading it from beginning to end rather than skipping around. In the meantime, if you ever get stuck, simply ask yourself: *What would Poe do?*

All the quotes that you'll find in the following chapters come from Poe himself, drawn from his letters, essays, poems, and stories, and all the lessons come from his life. As you'll see, far from being out of date, Poe's rueful, often cynical life-philosophy has stood the test of time. Take it from a man who is far more famous today than he ever was in his own lifetime—and who most definitely got the last laugh.

Now you can, too.

Poe's Most Important Poe Tip for You, Plus a Word about the French, Who Got Here First

The life-changing Poe-gram you're about to discover is, in fact, a proven formula. Simply consider the patient zero of Poe worship, Charles Baudelaire.

In 1847, the young French critic chanced upon Poe's story "The Black Cat" in a Parisian magazine, feeling an immediate, electric jolt of recognition. Somehow this mysterious American author had articulated the morbid sensations Baudelaire *also* experienced but could not put into words. When Baudelaire learned that Poe had been as broke and bad with money as himself, suffered from the same vices and received the same sort of critical scorn, he grew only more devoted. Though, at the time, Baudelaire had no precise grasp of English, he spent the next decade mastering the language so he could translate Poe's works into French, a task that spanned, all told, some seventeen years of his life. Baudelaire also published brilliant essays championing Poe as a martyr for the cause of beauty and truth, an existential hero. To this day, Poe is, in France, widely admired as a kind of debauched saint of the arts, while Baudelaire's translations are believed to be among the best literary translations *of all time*.

In his forties, near death, Baudelaire wrote in his journal: "I swear henceforth to observe the following rules as the eternal rules of my life. To pray every morning to God, source of all power and all justice; to my father . . . and to Poe as intercessors: to give me the strength necessary to accomplish all my duties." Syphilitic and destitute, he had nevertheless achieved fame as a genius writer with a terrible reputation, like his idol. How's that for a happy ending?

The more time I spend with Poe and his admirers, the more I realize how common this sense of Poe-as-personal-hero really is. People describe Poe as their literary first love, the writer who first demonstrated to them the ghastly, awesome "Power of Words," and the internet is full of fan art testifying to his effect on thousands of amateur poets, painters, and playwrights, plus countless tattooists. If you've been a faithful Poe fan for some years, then you already know the sway he can have, persuading you away from stable employment and encouraging you to crack on with your own doomed dreams.

Still, this aspect of Poe has—at least in America—mostly remained a matter of intuition, not spoken of or consciously understood. My goal here is to draw out that intuitive knowledge, dispense with *any* pretense of objectivity, elevate Poe to the dark lifestyle guru status he's always deserved, and ensure I receive "please seek help" emails for the rest of my life.*

Poe, if he had half a chance, would probably pan this book in his sneering signature style. I still like to think he'd approve of the impulse—not conventional self-help, but self-help told from the villain's perspective. *Anti*-self-help, if you will. Perhaps unsurprisingly, he did not much believe in progress. "I have no faith in human perfectibility," he told a friend. "Man is only now more active—not more happy—nor more wise, than he was 6000 years ago."

And late in his career, he wrote that if you want to find the genuinely intelligent, bold, brave, and exceptional people, you ought not to look in churches, nor to politicians—nor to Instagram influencers. While conceding that some individuals have most definitely "soared above the plane of their race," he said, "in looking back through history for traces of their existence, we should pass over all biographies of 'the good and the great,' while we search carefully the slight records of wretches who

---

* Speaking of objectivity and my receiving emails: This is a self-help book, not a complete or completely serious Poe biography; so, kids, don't quote me in your English papers, like "Baab-Muguira claims John Allan unfriended Poe on Venmo in 1831," or else you'll get a C.

died in prison, in Bedlam, or upon the gallows." He might as well have been endorsing himself. And you and me.

Being normal and well adjusted, as Poe knew, is nothing to brag about. Normal people spend their whole lives making cold calls to sell homeowners insurance. Normal people go into debt to buy jet skis and breast implants. Then they raise their children to do the same things. How much more rewarding is it to spend your life attempting to execute grandiose plans, and sometimes failing? You may have huge, glaring shortcomings, dire personality flaws, and a bizarre sex life that other people love to gossip about. But here in the Poe-verse, these are pros, not cons—features, not gold-bugs.

Traditionally, self-help kicks work like this: First, you get fed up with yourself. You feel off-course somehow, out of step with those efficient, chirpy beings around you (or in your feed), and so you resolve, with great earnestness, to *improve* yourself. To try keto, tone your core, and finish *War and Peace*, instead of, say, bingeing some '90s sitcom while scrolling Twitter and scarfing a Crunchwrap Supreme. It's a common yet dreadful error, this trying to better yourself. A shortcut to living a deeply conventional life. A meal-kit for feeling worse.

You're not going to discover the strength necessary to accomplish all your duties inside that copy of *How to Win Friends & Influence People*. You need to tap into a source at once darker, more demented, and radical, because my hunch is that what you want most in your heart of hearts is something much more valuable than happiness, peace, or satisfaction: the chance to realize your Poe-tential. That's why your *uber* Poe tip—the very essence of the Poe-gram, too fundamental even to be labeled number-one—is so simple, yet so crucial.

Stop looking for models of perfect living. Instead, embrace a brilliant visionary of terrible decisions to guide you to an epic life.

Got it? Excellent. Now for the rest of the Poe-gram.

PART I
Starting Out

To get you started on your journey to becoming more successful and more Poe-like, here's a glimpse into Poe's childhood and adolescence, the early formation of his contrarian ideas, and the very beginning of his distinguished career of misfitry. You'll discover how to:

- Locate the upside in your childhood pain

- Remain endlessly trapped in the past

- Capitalize on your youthful egotism (and neurotic mistrust!)

Plus so much more—no matter how young, old, or undead you may be.

Lose Early, Lose Often

In November of 1811, a brief notice appeared in the *Richmond Enquirer*:

> *TO THE HUMANE HEART*
> On this night, *Mrs. Poe*, lingering on the bed of disease and
> surrounded by her children, asks your *assistance*; and
> *asks it perhaps for the last time.* The generosity of a Richmond
> Audience can need no other appeal.

It was the sad end of a charming career. Eliza Poe had been acting professionally since the age of nine, and in her fifteen years on the stage had played Juliet, Desdemona, Ophelia, and Cordelia, all the great Shakespearean heroines. She excelled at light comedy and could sing and dance, too: a triple threat. Critics raved. Men swooned.

The single portrait of her that survives shows a big-eyed, bosomy girl-child with dark curls, dangling earrings, and a dress cut low enough to catch your eye. "She was said to be one of the handsomest women in America; she was certainly the handsomest woman I had ever seen," one fan swore. "She never came on the Stage, but a general murmur ran through the house, 'What an enchanting Creature! Heavens, what a form!'"

Now Eliza lay dying in a shabby room in Richmond, Virginia, not far from the theater where she'd so recently performed. Her husband, David Poe, had abandoned her, disappearing sometime before she gave birth to a little girl. No one remained nearby to care for her children—Henry, aged four years, Edgar, aged two, and the infant, Rosalie—except theater friends and some kind locals, who brought fresh bedclothes and little baskets of food, trying to tempt Eliza to eat. But the struggle for breath occupied her most. Tuberculosis means drowning inside your own body. Your lungs liquefy, then you choke on the fluid.

With her strength almost gone, Eliza put aside a few small tokens for each of her children. She took a hand-size painting she'd done of Boston

Harbor and, on the reverse side, inscribed a few lines "for my little son Edgar" in a lilting hand. It was almost all she had to leave him.

As an adult, Edgar Allan Poe would say he could not remember either of his biological parents. Not his beautiful mother. Not his glum, hard-drinking, self-pitying father, David, who, in the age-old tradition, seems to have been not quite the equal of his wife. Nevertheless, some impression lingered. If you've been around very young children any length of time, you know that they absorb and perceive far more than we ever give them credit for. The verbal ones remember the snarky things you said to your friend on the phone, and then they repeat it all later, in company. The preverbal ones can be harder to gauge, but their inability to articulate their feelings doesn't mean they don't have feelings.

Early childhood is a time of rage and despair, and that's for the fortunate kids who *don't* experience trauma. You're intensely vulnerable. Utterly dependent. Your needs—for love, attention, instruction, mashed peas, and *Paw Patrol*—are greater than at any other time in your life. The architecture of your brain is still forming, and all the forms of chronic stress present in your early environment can find their way into the structure of how you'll think and feel for the rest of your life. Meanwhile, you asked for precisely none of this. No one consulted you before you were thrust from the creamy peace of the womb into life, with its humidity and injustice and coupons that turn out not to work when you actually want to use them.

For kids who do experience trauma, there's the added difficulty of somehow processing profound emotional pain—something that grown-ups with driver's licenses and office jobs can barely handle. It's not easier on children simply because they're smaller, whatever adults may want to believe. While debate raged for the last hundred-plus years, today's psychologists generally agree that a young child may experience grief as powerfully as you and I do. The loss of one's mother in particular, the child-development researcher Sir John Bowlby wrote, can cause "grief and mourning of an intensity which can dislocate the development of his personality." And reactions may run the gamut: the bereaved child might make "unreasonable demands." He might, at the same time, become "irritable and ungrateful to those who try to respond."

We love to hear about people's secrets of success. Like: Hey, bro, how'd you get those eight-pack abs? How'd you grow your home business into a billion-dollar enterprise? How'd you become a celebrated, world-changing author, beloved by millions for your nightmare visions and infinitely sad, dirge-like poems?

About 99 percent of the time, the answers seem sanitized, bowdlerized, as though a *Fast Company* or TED Talk audience couldn't handle the truth. You hear single buzzword responses like "focus" and "determination." Or people detail their bizarre wellness routines, like waking up at four a.m. every day, or fasting six days a week, or whatever this week's abstemious health trend consists of. Nobody speaks of the underlying psychology that gives rise to such marked traits and habits. Nobody ever says, "I'm propelled along almost unconsciously by the most incredible, profound grief." Nobody ever tells you that early loss can exert a massive, lifelong effect, ensuring you become a person whose single overriding goal is to climb the highest hill there is so that you can scream "What the *FUCK*!!!!" from the top.

But this kind of misshapen mindset goes a long way toward explaining Poe's literary career, as well as a great many other distinguished careers, literary and otherwise.

It may be deeply offensive to suggest there could be any magical silver lining to childhood pain. No sane person would wish for any child, anywhere, to suffer. Nor is it wise, however, to dismiss the notion that some upside could still emerge. Horrendous emotional pain, though undesirable, a thing no one would choose, *can* be a powerful motivator. It may even be a force of nature. My personal suspicion is that humans have evolved to feel as though we should make sense of our pain somehow, in the same way we feel strangely compelled to find uses for stale bread or driftwood.

Viktor Frankl, the Auschwitz survivor and pioneering psychiatrist, saw the drive for meaning as key to our survival, while the psychologist Bruno Bettelheim once wrote, "Our greatest need and most difficult achievement is to find meaning in our lives," describing this process as no less urgent in childhood than in adulthood. Early loss can be a spur, getting you started on the task of finding meaning long before your peers ever feel any existential itch. It can inspire you to ask the really big, cosmic questions (such as "Are you kidding me?"). And it can encourage you to seek greater knowledge and to develop the linguistic skills you need to describe your inner condition.

In this way, an early experience of profound pain may be *the* most important qualification you could have for a future creative career. Even better, it's free. Pain is available and in great supply. You've undoubtedly got some just lying around loose, or in dusty old boxes deep in your psyche, left over like 8-bit Nintendo cartridges or parched Play-Doh from your childhood. Why not go digging?

Now, you may be thinking, "But I never had it as bad as the young Edgar Allan Poe." Don't sell yourself short! It's not important that you experience loss on Poe's precise level. Very few of us are in his league that way. Most of us have only run-of-the-mill bad childhoods, with our parents' marriage exploding in acrimony and recrimination, or an older sibling helpfully deciding that competing with us and humiliating us is their *raison d'être*. Anyway, chances are some things happened you were pretty damn unhappy with.

Almost all of us experience the usual rage inducers:

- ➤ You probably found, like most of us find, that after a certain initial period (and far too early for your taste) you were no longer "the baby."

- ➤ Likewise, you probably found that your every whim would not be catered to, that you could not control others with the simple force of your will—that those meanie adults were going to deny your desires no matter how you beat your tiny fists on the laminate.

- ➤ At some point, you may have also discovered you were not born into the vast material wealth you would've preferred. That, without a choice in the matter, you were going to have to watch other children enjoy toys, activities, and individually wrapped snacks you would not be enjoying yourself.

You may be fifteen or fifty as you read this, but the point remains the same. Whatever happened to you, the important thing is to never achieve closure. Do not endeavor to get over your childhood pain— instead, concentrate on it. Keep the horror close. And, of course, this is to say almost nothing of the vast array of *other*, nonpersonal problems and cruelties you first notice when you're a kid, but that don't directly affect your life. Don't take your focus off those, either. There are people who look around this world and think everything is fine. And the nicest possible thing you can say about them is: they are not us. You've probably heard Dylan Thomas's dictum: "Rage, rage against the dying of the light." Except why limit yourself? Why not rage against the dawning of the light, too? Once you open your tiny, puffy little infant eyes and the rough outline of the setup on planet Earth starts to become clear, you should never, ever stop objecting.

Take it from Poe. This is a guy, remember, who at forty was still writing about childhood, and who essentially spent his whole career coming up with a word for never again seeing the person whom you love most. You have to admire his stamina, the way he never made peace with anything, or shut up about it. It's an example to us all.

Poe tip #1: Don't just complain. Howl like an infant.

Try test-driving the affirmations on the next page, and see if they don't help you recall some lost, forgotten tinglings of outrage. Or skip to Lesson #2 (see page 10) to discover why it's good news you're so hopelessly neurotic.

Repeat After Poe:
Affirmations for the Enraged Infant in All of Us

←——————————●——————————→

Wail the following sayings out loud, first thing in the morning and last thing at night. Even better, scrawl them in crayon on your wall.

1. The world has irreparably wronged me. I will burn it down.

2. My heart is forever broken. Closure is a lie.

3. They. Will. Pay.

4. I am everything. I form the very center of the world. Nothing exists outside me.

5. There's no way my parents could have spawned someone so fascinating and advanced. I must've been adopted.

Embracing Your Inner Neurotic

After your father dips out and your mother has the audacity to die on you, here are a few experiences that might cause alarm and anxiety in a little kid or, really, in anyone:

- ➤ Being suddenly separated from your siblings—before you've even had the chance to learn to hate them.

- ➤ Being plunked down in a new environment alone, among strangers, and told these people are your new family. Like *Home Alone 2*, except a lot less fun.

- ➤ Moving to a foreign country where your *new* family falls apart, and then being sent away *again*, to live among more strangers, so that you effectively lose everything yet one more time.

All of which happened to Poe. In the last weeks of his mother Eliza Poe's life, the well-to-do ladies of Richmond adopted her as a charity case, and following her death, when decisions were being made about what would become of her orphaned children, one of the ladies decided to take Edgar into her home. The woman's name was Frances Allan, and she had no children of her own. In 1803, she'd married Scottish immigrant and hard-charging businessman John Allan, but eight years in, their nursery remained empty. Little Edgar would become the Allans' ward, if not quite their son.

Edgar was in taller cotton now—doted upon by his affluent foster parents and dressed in tiny suits "like a young prince," according to biographer Eugene L. Didier. So you might assume his days of worrying were over. Well.

While John Allan's trading business was prosperous, he still nursed an ambition to expand across the Atlantic, and in 1815, he seized the chance, moving the family to London, England. However, Frances hated boat travel and London, too. She soon grew ill, with vague yet unremitting symptoms that today read, at least in part, as clinical depression. Then John's fledgling new operation tanked with the broad recession spreading throughout Europe. Instead of hightailing it, he dug in, while Frances spent weeks away from home, recuperating in villages on the coast, where the air was said to be better. Their sniping letters back and forth—John implying that Frances was malingering, Frances implying John enjoyed himself more when she was gone—do not suggest the couple had much time for the six-year-old who called them "Pa" and "Ma." In fact, they'd packed little Edgar off to boarding school.

If you set out to create history's most accomplished neurotic, you could do a lot worse than to combine this intermittent, uncertain kind of nurture with Edgar's peculiar kind of nature. Poe would, in his thirties, use one of the institutions he was sent to as the setting in "William Wilson," a story about a boy whose wealthy upbringing gives way to grave suspicion when, on his first day at boarding school, he meets another boy exactly like himself. To encounter one's self is uncomfortable, Poe hints. Even terrifying.

Deeply neurotic people like you and me will recognize his meaning intuitively, twitchy stress-smiles appearing on our faces. Self-consciousness,

self-doubt, self-questioning, and self-blame are the hallmarks of our condition, so we know what it is to conceive of the self as a problem. *The* problem. No matter our backgrounds or our circumstances, we tend to think whatever is wrong must stem from some internal source—as though our lives were a horror movie in which the call is always coming from inside the house.

"Neuroses" is an old term now, known in Poe's day but phased out of textbooks and diagnostic manuals some forty years ago. These days, psychologists tend to see neuroticism as a set of traits, strongly present or weakly present, rather than an overriding condition. According to the

Big 5 model of personality, it's a spectrum: Everyone may be a little bit neurotic, with some people more neurotic than others. Neurotic characteristics include not just self-doubt and self-blame, but also extreme sensitivity, shyness, nervousness, fearfulness, moodiness, paranoia, and being kind of intense, kind of a lot. All these traits are identifiable in children as young as toddlers, as my mom will assure you.

Another aspect of the strongly neurotic personality, somehow left out of official definitions, is a sense of being different from those around you, of being "Alone."* Perhaps, from the time you were a little kid, you've been aware of a gulf between yourself and others made up of something more fundamental than inequalities of social class or natural talent—an odd quality in yourself you never quite had a name for.

Perhaps you had thoughts that did not occur to your fellow third-graders, and a lot of those thoughts were unpleasant. Perhaps once or twice you got a little bee in your brain about the fact that we're all just spinning out in empty space billions of freezing miles from the next unknowable swirl of gas and rock and no one knows why, there's just no explanation, no satisfactory answer—like was it some angry, vindictive god who did this, or was it, even more horrifyingly, sheer chance? And what would happen if you could somehow reach the end of the universe: Would you just cease to exist or instead run smack into a wall of knotty pine? Maybe, from an early age, you were a reader.

You might not, on the surface, see this kind of personality—Poe's type of personality, our type of personality—as desirable. And if your

---

* This is the Poe poem that begins, "From childhood's hour, I have not been / as others were," prompting many of us to nod along, like, "Oh yeah, man. Same."

adult reading has deteriorated (like mine) to self-help books, you know that you're supposed to try your damnedest to change. You need to shut down and reboot, the workbooks and podcasts say. Reset your mindset. Stop overthinking everything like a loser, and instead "fuel like a winner" as Dwight Schrute might put it, or seek to "awaken the giant within" per Tony Robbins. And hell, sometimes it's tempting to listen to them. You've already spent great swathes of your life feeling unaccountably down, staring into the abyss so long it not only stares back at you but winks like a creep. You're probably sick of vacillating, considering, reconsidering. Angsting.

The good news is, there's at least *one* thing you can stop worrying about right now. Your tendencies to anxiety and overthinking are strengths, not weaknesses. What's more, you *want* to stand out from the herd of well-adjusted, nonpsychotic humans. The company is much better, for one. Some of the most successful people who ever lived were neurotic messes, Poe not least of them.

Plus, it's freeing to stop trying to be normal. Think about it for three seconds and you'll realize that normalcy is a trap, a kind of bogus psychological credit score that society demands of us but which smart people refuse to care about. Having met at least a few of your fellow humans, you know this to be fact: no one is normal, not really. The world can be divided into people who are complete neurotics and *don't* know it, and people who are complete neurotics and *do* know it.

You are one of the lucky, enlightened ones, aware of your neuroses and so capable of putting this crap to good use. No longer must you laboriously attempt to identify as a good friend, faithful employee, and solid, tax-paying citizen who has never once lied on a pet-adoption form or snuck a handful of fancy cashews out of the bulk bins at the grocery store. Instead, you're free to chew on things, overanalyze, daydream, invent, and create, breaking all those stupid old rules, just like the long line of neurotics who preceded you and are responsible for virtually everything interesting that has ever happened.

Wisdom, the ancient Greeks said, starts with "know thyself." Most people don't know thyselves well at all. Yet you know what you are—and have the privilege of seeing yourself amid some of history's most distinctive personalities. Cast your eye over the brief list below.

Abraham Lincoln and Mary Todd Lincoln: The sixteenth president, who helped end slavery in the United States, suffered melancholic episodes from his teenage years on. Mary, his wife and the mother of their four sons, was declared mentally incompetent late in life and spent months in an asylum. Only by publicly embarrassing her family was she able to secure her release.

Franz Kafka: The deeply depressed author of *The Metamorphosis*—office jobber wakes up as cockroach-like creature—suffered an endless string of psychosomatic complaints, from insomnia to headaches, constipation to hemorrhoids. Oh Mylanta! Kafka was, arguably, too neurotic even to finish his ingenious novels, although they were, nevertheless, published after his death.

Louis E. Bisch: A professor at the New York Polyclinic Medical School and Hospital, Bisch wrote the fantastic but now sadly forgotten self-help title *Be Glad You're Neurotic*, which was first published in 1936 and will make for rewarding further reading if this lesson speaks to you. ("Being neurotic has enriched my life and given a zest to what otherwise might have been routine existence," the good doctor explains. "25/10 would do it again.")

Marilyn Monroe: Movie star and proof, alongside me, that even the most beautiful, alluring women may be neurotic. Earned the love of the whole world and found it wasn't enough—a neurotic level few others ever manage to unlock. Drank, took pills, maybe slept with two different Kennedys, and still did brilliant work in comedies.

Warren Zevon: Singer-songwriter who famously ran out on his tab at the Hollywood Hawaiian Hotel with the aid of one of the Beach Boys. Enjoyed issues with depression, OCD, and alcoholism, helpfully taking it all out on his young family. Once told the *New York Times*, "Sometimes I think I get headaches from analyzing my headaches."

A long, long list of rap artists: From DMX to Biggie to Eminem among the old-schoolers, to Lil Peep and Lil Uzi Vert more recently. Soundcloud rap, still one of the most popular genres as of this writing, is more or less explicitly *about* anxiety and the only semi-recreational use of Xanax.

In short, there are others; they are your fellows, your peeps, and together they make a helpful point. The only way out is through. What you want is not to deny or avoid or suppress the neurotic aspects of your personality, but rather *to seek to activate your neuroses at a far greater level.*

Poe said as much himself, in one of those passages in his work that is supposed to be fiction, but it's like he's breaking the fourth wall and speaking directly to the camera: "Men have called me mad; but the question is not yet settled, whether madness is or is not the loftiest intelligence—whether much that is glorious—whether all that is profound—does not spring from disease of thought. . . ."

Seek the profound and glorious. Harness your unique combination of messed-up nature and screwed-up nurture, and find some problem to attack that is outside yourself. Any field of human endeavor will do: math, science, medicine, art, music, literature, crosswords, CrossFit, coding, knitting. Doesn't matter. You just need an outlet. And boy, does the Poe-gram have a deal for you! Just see the next lesson.

Poe tip #2: Why be basic? Cultivate the conflicted, overthinking, anxious mess you already are.

Hubris, or How to Begin Your Life's Work

Beginning around age ten or eleven, children experience vast hormonal changes that result in the appearance of secondary sexual characteristics as well as a host of awkward feelings. Along with the pubic hair, they get the angst. And along with the angst, some of them get an overriding desire to express their feelings in verse.

In *terrible* verse, like Poe did.

When the Allan family sailed back across the Atlantic in 1820, resettling in Richmond, Virginia, Edgar was eleven years old, right on the precipice of that long period of physical, cognitive, and psychological changes that in his day was simply known as "youth," but nowadays is called adolescence. Edgar was also, once again, the new kid in school. John Allan had enrolled him at one of the best local schools around—a private boys' academy run by headmaster Joseph H. Clarke.

One day, not long after Edgar started classes, John Allan showed up at the academy carrying a sheaf of papers that today might be worth hundreds of thousands, perhaps millions, of dollars—if only it hadn't been lost. This was Edgar Allan Poe's first poetry manuscript, perhaps the only copy that ever existed. And John Allan's question for Clarke was straightforward: Did he think these poems ought to be published?

Clarke thought it over. Edgar "possessed a great deal of self-esteem" already, he said. It wouldn't do for the boy to be "flattered and talked about as the author of a printed book at his age."

The verses, Clarke would recall, "consisted chiefly of pieces addressed to the different little girls in Richmond." But because the manuscript was lost, none of those pieces are available to us now. We can only guess something of their quality from the very first lines of Poe's that do survive, and that appear to date from a few years later.

> Last night, with many cares & toils oppress'd,
> Weary, I laid me on a couch to rest –

It's just a fragment of a poem, one that the young Poe was apparently too weary to ever finish, and yet it's all there—the self-seriousness, the clumsy rhyme, the heavy sigh of adolescence rising off the page like fog off a fetid pond. With some slight changes to capture modern diction, the lines would be at home in any tween journal—maybe your journal?—today. Frankly, all that makes this couplet remarkable is the fact that it wasn't Poe's last—that he kept writing, and eventually became a much better poet.

Even Poe's first book, *Tamerlane and Other Poems*, which he published anonymously at age eighteen, sank like a kettlebell in the ocean when it first appeared. No one at the time caught any whiff of genius. No one started tossing around terms like "prodigy" and "wunderkind." Hell, no one seems to have read the thing at all when it first came out. Still, if you're ever at a flea market and come across a small, faded, cheaply bound pamphlet written by "A Bostonian," be sure you snap it up. Only about fifty copies of *Tamerlane* were printed, just a dozen or so remain extant today, and in 2009 one sold for $662,500—setting a new record for a work of American literature at auction.

For hundreds of years, artists, scientists, and Malcolm Gladwell have debated whether geniuses are born or made. Does innate talent or diligent practice matter more? Can 10,000 hours of dedicated cramming really transform a rando into a Beatle or an NBA baller? Eh, maybe. In Poe's case, his artistic genes, his early life with his theatrical parents, and his fancy, language-focused education all help to explain his later achievement, and must matter at least as much as the hours of scrawling he began putting in as a youth. Yet it's possible we're still overlooking the most important aspect of his development: What if the "great deal of self-esteem" the young Poe possessed was the secret to his eventual success?

Poe himself phrased the question this way: "When did ever Ambition exist or Talent prosper without prior conviction of success?" In his formulation, "conviction of success" comes *before* ambition, *before* talent.

Self-esteem + conviction of success > talent + ambition

The same goes for you. In your own path to an epic, Poe-like life, it's not enough to be obsessively mournful and incredibly neurotic. You're going to need a good deal more *oomph* to get you over the gap between your inevitably humble, juvenile beginnings and your eventual triumph. And the best source of that *oomph* is unreasonable, extravagant, Poe-like self-esteem (i.e., hubris).*

Of course, this advice slaps the face of thousands of years of Western thought. The Greeks saw hubris as a fatal flaw that could bring about

---

* You could also call it "interminable pride," as Poe did in one of the *Tamerlane* poems.

even a great hero's downfall. Jews and early Christians weren't too hot on excessive self-confidence, either. "Pride goeth before destruction," warns the Old Testament, "and an haughty spirit before a fall." The New Testament is likewise peppered with statements on the desirability of a humble nature and putting others before ourselves.

But maybe you're not so much aiming to enter the Kingdom of Heaven right now as you are attempting to join the ranks of the famous, the powerful, and the highly paid. Pride goeth before earthly achievement, too, as Poe knew, and a haughty spirit can beget a rise. Whatever you see as your life's work, it's crucial to set out from a place of overconfidence.

Overcompensation is the operative idea, as is an inaccurate estimate of your capacity for excellence. No matter your chosen field, the task ahead of you is so daunting, so complex and huge, that if you really knew what you were getting into you'd probably never get started at all. This is all the more true if you've ever been encouraged to know your place and stay in your lane.

Are you:

- Young, and everyone's telling you you're too young?

- A lonely teenager desperate to survive until adulthood and freedom?

- A twenty-something struggling to find your footing (and a job and a partner and a place to live that you don't hate)?

- A midlife wage slave staring down decades of some forty-hour-a-week grind?

- Supposedly over the hill and worried that trying anything new will make you look ridiculous?

Well, then. Take it from Poe: you need to go ahead and get high on your own supply. Get proud, get downright arrogant, and get ready to become exceptional. It doesn't matter if other people think you're a no-talent ass-clown, à la *Office Space*. You must believe you have inordinate ability, that you are more than qualified, only baby steps away from greatness. Go beyond the usual cutting yourself a break and *actively give yourself credit you don't deserve*. Don't deserve yet, anyway.

The trick of it is to hide your excessive self-belief from your teachers, your parents, your bosses, your friends—lest they try to prevent you from publishing your terrible poems or auditioning for Broadway just because you can't carry a tune. Far better to tune out *their* voices. Encouragement is always better coming from within than without, and not least because other people's pesky feelings might get in the way. Do the people who would bring you down, who tell you to be meek and humble, *really* have your best interests at heart?

Given the chance, plenty of people will discourage you for no better reason than because *they* were discouraged—and they're still discouraged now. Sometimes, too, there's a widespread cultural belief in not getting ahead of yourself, as exemplified in the "tall poppy syndrome" thought to pervade former British colonies. Essentially, it's a society-wide diktat that says the tall poppy will get chopped down. Or, put in American English, *You think you're better than me, huh? Huh?!* But the syndrome isn't just confined to New Zealand and Singapore. It may be present in your family culture, your school culture, your church culture, your work culture, and/or your shitty-sublet-with-nine-roommates culture.

Kept secret, hubris is a kind of lightness of step. It lets you feel vindicated ahead of time, to imagine your own first book of poems one day setting new records at auction. It offers the same thrill you get from imagining how regretful and ashamed folks will be—weeping, wringing their hands, gnashing their teeth—at your funeral. You can luxuriate in vengeful fantasies of your frenemies being given the news, of everyone in your crappy hometown finding out at once that you are actually among the world's greatest at—well, whatever you're going to be among the world's greatest at. In hindsight, they'll all see it. They'll all have seen it all along.

Poe tip #3: Do not attempt to rein in your own bullshit. Buy wholeheartedly into your deepest self-delusions and take outrageous pride in your work— no matter who denigrates it.

Hindsight, not coincidentally, seems to have helped make Poe's early talent clear to his headmaster, Clarke. "While the other boys wrote mere mechanical verses, Poe wrote genuine poetry: the boy was a born poet," Clarke told those who came searching for anecdotes from Poe's school days. Which may've been true to some extent, sure, but was all too easy to say years after Poe's death, by which time he was widely acknowledged to be a genius. Way to bet on the winning horse, bucko, the day after the goddang race!

Good thing Poe had so much hubris that he never required Clarke's approval. If he had, you might not be reading this now, or be on your *own* stealth march to greatness.

Identifying Your Massive Poe-tential

Not yet sure what department of human endeavor may contain your life's work? What are five to ten things that you are incredibly good at, just not yet? Neurosurgery? Dressage? Don't think small. Let your "great deal of self-esteem" be your guide.

Chip on Your Shoulder? Good!

Ludlam's Wharf on the James River, Richmond, Virginia, June 1824. Another boy bets the fifteen-year-old Poe that he can't swim all the way to Warwick, a site some seven and a half miles distant. So, under a bright sun, against a powerful tide chugging along at three knots, Edgar swims the entire length, and when he reaches his goal, he offers to breaststroke all the way back, too.

He's not even out of breath, and yet he's set a new record for the city, the country, even the world. Not only does he win the bet and embarrass those bastards who doubted him, the Richmond papers run news of the feat, and the story becomes a local legend, spoken of for generations. Well into Poe's thirties, no one else in town—or across the globe—can best his record.

Poe was still repeating this tale to friends and magazine profilers decades later—and, it's possible, feeding them lines into the bargain. Writer Henry B. Hirst, who put together an early biography of Poe based on notes that *Poe himself provided*, described the swim as "fully equal to 30 miles in still water," and so "Herculean" that it "has never been equaled by anyone, properly authenticated."

The problem comes when you try to authenticate *Poe's* story.

➤ It's not a distance of seven and a half miles from the wharf to Warwick. More like five.*

➤ Poe's route was from west to east, downriver. Around Richmond, the James rises and falls with the tide, but it does not *reverse course*, as Hirst's biography implies. And five miles with the current carrying you along does not equal thirty miles in still water, no matter how you stroke the facts.

➤ While there were witnesses to swear the swim *did* occur, it does not appear to have been covered in any newspapers at the time, like Poe insisted.

You may wonder: What kind of person inflates their teenage accomplishments like this? What kind of person goes so far in their exaggeration that they *claim to have set a world record*?† A person who is excessively vain, overly ambitious, and at the same time deeply insecure. Someone like Poe, that is—and if you're lucky, like you, too.

On the face of it, a gnawing sense of your own inadequacy might seem incompatible with the outsized self-esteem discussed in the last lesson, but nothing could be further from the truth. When you combine being utterly full of yourself *with* having a massive chip on your shoulder, that's when you get the trademark Poe rocket fuel. *Boom goes the dynamite.*

---

* Poe (writing elsewhere) said it was six miles, while Google Maps puts it closer to four. And it must be said that this hyped-up swimming anecdote is only one of many embellishments, if not outright whoppers, that Poe apparently fed Hirst.

† Me.

We all know being born into privilege is a serious advantage. It's not such a big deal to get into Harvard if your family's name is etched onto the edifice of the library. It's not as difficult to get your own TV show, or a job at Goldman Sachs, or the money to develop an app when you come from a long line of people with TV shows, Wall Street careers, and spare stacks of cash. And yet, often as not, children from posh circumstances fail to accomplish anything. They grow up to become drunks and addicts, ne'er-do-wells, gadflies, layabouts, president of the United States. They rarely feel a need to excel or question whether they deserve everything they have. Their privilege renders them blind, deaf and dumb, complacent, just as they are.

Poe, however, was arguably far more fortunate. He got to enjoy the fancy clothes, international travel, servants (i.e., slaves), and pricey schooling that life with the Allans afforded him. He was in their world, yet, crucially, not of it. Richmond isn't a buzzing metropolis now, and it was even smaller, more insular and prattling in Poe's day, with a population of just about 12,000, only a bit more than half of whom were free citizens. Rumors of his shameful low origins made the rounds, then made the rounds again. Actresses such as Eliza Poe—however talented or popular they might be—were little better than whores, after all, and actors were hardly more respectable. Meanwhile, Poe's classmates could count themselves as the biological sons of some of Virginia's "best" families: the gentleman farmers, businessmen, judges, doctors, and their society wives.

You can bet Poe felt that difference, and that it rankled. In the grand tradition of teenagers everywhere, his fellow students weren't going to let him forget it, either.

"Of Edgar Poe it was known that his parents were players, and that he was dependent upon the bounty that is bestowed upon an adopted son," classmate J. T. L. Preston would recall, decades after their school days ended. "All this had the effect of making the boys decline his leadership; and on looking back on it since, I fancy it gave him a fierceness he would otherwise not have had."

This "fierceness" became Poe's unwelcome windfall—a gift-in-disguise sense of grievance that encouraged him to take up silly swimming bets, to box and run competitively, to perform at the top of his class, and compulsively achieve, achieve, achieve. And, of course, exaggerate his achievements. Poe would *always* feel a powerful desire to outperform and dominate his peers, and he remained, until his death, an unreliable source of information about his own accomplishments. Who could blame him? Besides, it only *served* him. We don't know the names of any of those rich jerks from his school, except to the extent they had something to say about *him*. But Poe? He now has four different museums dedicated to his memory.

Until now, you may have felt slightly ashamed at the way you resent your family, your town, your background—perhaps you even resent *yourself* for being so constantly disgruntled and aggrieved. Society first fills you full of resentment, then blithely tells you to let go of it. What a load of crap. As Poe's example shows, resentment is not just a performance-enhancing drug, it's damn near a miracle—like steroids without the acne, shrunken testicles, or string of ill-advised sequels.

Understanding why is no great leap. Those who feel like they've got something to prove will work harder and longer at whatever task, in whatever situation has ignited their sense of personal inadequacy. They'll run more practice laps. Complete more practice tests. They don't need Wheaties because their emotional hunger is in control, and insecurity is the real breakfast of champions. Though they may get tired, they won't stop—they'll keep going till they collapse. Then they'll get up again the next day, earlier than the competition.

Energy has to come from somewhere, and resentment is a renewable resource. The more you stew, the more you dwell on it, the more you have! If we could somehow figure out how to charge the electrical grid with resentment, we probably could stop climate change right now, keep those glaciers from melting into Greek yogurt. Make no mistake: alongside hubris, a deep-seated sense of personal grievance is one of the most powerful forces on earth. It can reverse the course of rivers, increase distances by as much as 50 percent, *and* invent fawning newspaper stories wholesale.

Most life advice says you ought to focus on the positive and put the negative aside, by "practicing gratitude." The suggestion here is only slightly different, a kind of clever hack—to practice gratitude *for your grievances*. Count that chip on your shoulder as a blessing, not a curse. Not fortunate enough to have a fully formed one? Then stop whatever you're doing and start nurturing your chip. Pour on the Miracle Gro and watch the spider plant expand to occupy the whole living room of your mind. Ask yourself: What real or imagined disadvantages could you obsess about even more, starting today, starting *right now*?

As your chip grows over time, over the months and years and decades, all this focus and obsession will mean you end up being exceedingly skilled in your field. I mean, yeah, it's also true that an uncontrolled grievance may push every other good thing out of your life, interfering with your ability to maintain friendships and romances. But no source of motivation is perfect. Whoever said intense psychological drive necessarily arrives in pure, healthy form? Given what we know about evolution, it makes much more sense that our motivation would be at least as improvised and makeshift as the spine or the eyeball, both of which also work in what at first glance seem like totally haphazard ways.

Maybe you grew up on the wrong side of the tracks. Or maybe you just felt like you did, everything being relative. Maybe you grew up in the family with the least amount of money of anyone in your froufrou planned community, then you went to a state university and graduated only to discover that the profession you hoped to enter is essentially closed to all but alumni of the Ivy League and those who can afford to work lengthy unpaid internships in New York (hi!). Maybe you were physically undersized or oversized, and the other kids were cruel. Maybe you have a learning disability and struggled in class even though you were smarter than everyone there, Miss Bunn included.

The world has a million ways of doing us wrong and dicking us over. You know who else had a chip on their shoulder? Poe is only the top of the list. There's a long intellectual pedigree to being a resentful mofo. The roll call of incredibly accomplished people who were righteously, *rightfully* aggrieved, typically from childhood on, is at least five miles long, maybe even seven and a half—including Martin Luther, Charles Dickens, Louisa May Alcott, Malcolm X—and on and on. Every one of them had a little voice whispering in their ear about the times they were rejected, oppressed, misjudged, mistreated, brutalized, and abused . . . and the world is better for it. Listen well, and your chip will speak to you, too.

Poe tip #4: Don't waste your life trying to overcome your resentment. Cherish that chip on your shoulder. Treat it like your own personal raven.

All you have to do is put your resentment to intelligent ends, which means finding worthy objects of your ambition, useful candidates for competition. It's important to aim high. While we're young, we tend to look only to those immediately around us—in our social circle, in our suburb—but to satisfy your adult ego, you need to find a bigger stage and a grander setting. More on this in the next lesson. Complete the exercise on the next page, and we'll move on (without, obviously, *really* moving on).

A Grievance Gratitude Exercise

Below, recall the grievances you are grateful for *and* useful grievances you may've foolishly abandoned.

- Name the top five most humiliating experiences in your life. What do they have in common? Can you recall any other memories that make you unconsciously curl your hands into fists, clench your jaw, and grind your teeth?

- Who are some people you've resented over the years? If consequences didn't exist and you'd never have to listen to them tediously defend themselves, who would you call up and tell off right now?

- What activities bring out your obsessive competitive streak? Why? How could you incorporate more of these activities into your daily routine?

- Extra Credit: Make three wild claims about your life that can neither be confirmed nor disproved.

Dealing with Rejection
(and Vowing Your Revenge)

When Edgar Allan Poe was seventeen years old, he and John Allan loaded up the family station wagon with all his clothes, posters, and books, and made the seventy-mile trek west to Charlottesville, Virginia. Among the rolling hills of that town, Thomas Jefferson had recently founded a university meant to serve the sons of the state—at least, those sons who could afford to spend a few years drinking, gambling, goofing off, and, on occasion, attending the odd lecture, maybe sitting an exam or two. Poe saw his own place in these ranks, and longed to distinguish himself in this fresh social and academic setting.

He may have been glad to leave Richmond for other reasons, too. Poe's teenage years had seen a certain tension crop up in his relationship with his foster father. Gone were the relative ease, affection, and approval—if not intimacy—of their relations when Poe was still a child. At some point, Poe probably learned of the illegitimate children that John Allan had fathered elsewhere in Richmond, which may have been what prompted Allan to insist that the rumors about Poe's biological *mother* were true—that Eliza's youngest child had been fathered by another man, not her husband.

Writing to Poe's brother, Henry, in 1824, John Allan pointedly referred to Rosalie as "half your Sister," adding piously, in case his point was somehow missed, "God forbid my dear Henry that We should visit upon the living the Errors & frailties of the dead." In the same letter, he complained that Poe "does nothing & seems quite miserable, sulky & ill-tempered to all the Family." John Allan was, it seems, beginning to resent his ward's reliance on his charity—as in, how come this assetless teenage orphan just accepted everything he was given? Why couldn't he pull himself up by his bootstraps like John Allan had? Sure, John Allan was, about this time, being bailed out of a tough spot by his wealthy uncle—whose fortune he would soon inherit—but even so, *he* had never enjoyed the kind of advantages Poe enjoyed. *He* had never had the chance to go to college.

If Poe relished his escape from these harangues, he may have also realized that he was being set up to fail. Before leaving him in Charlottesville in February of 1826, John Allan handed Poe just $110 (or so Poe would claim later). This when tuition and fees ran closer to $350.

You know how it goes. You're on your own for the first time. You don't want to admit how lost you are, don't want to beg or turn back the way you came. And so, to cover the widening gap between your means and your expenses, you start to borrow. If there had been, in those days, credit-card company reps loitering outside the UVA student union with their quills and free waistcoats, Poe would have signed up on the spot.

As it was, he first cadged some credit from merchants in town, and when that proved not quite enough, he tossed back a couple of peach brandies and sat down at the poker table, cracking his knuckles and hoping for the best. After a few hands, he found himself in an even bigger hole, so he just kept on playing and losing, and losing, and losing, until he was $2,000 in hock—some $50,000 in today's money.

Now he *really* couldn't stay in Charlottesville. There was nothing for it but to trudge home, tail between his legs, creditors nipping at his heels.

John Allan gloated, hard, as bullies do. All he would offer Poe was an unpaid job in one of his offices. He refused to pay Poe's debts, and when collection agents arrived at the ornate family manse, attempting to seize Poe's possessions, they found there was nothing to repo—no TV, no Xbox, much less a Corolla. Foster father and foster son argued bitterly, and Poe decided to quit John Allan's house before he was pushed, or perhaps *as* he was pushed. He left the manse, retreating to who knows where, and swearing to John Allan in a letter that he would find "some place in this wide world, where I will be treated—not as *you* have treated me."

In this same kiss-off of a letter, Poe requested that John Allan send him some starting-out money, as well as his trunk and clothes. His foster father did not reply. The next day, Poe wrote again, his tone turning desperate. "I am in the greatest necessity, not having tasted food since Yesterday morning," he admitted, abandoning his earlier bravado. "I have no where to sleep at night, but roam about the Streets – I am nearly exhausted. . . ."

Once upon a time, rejection by one's tribe was a literal death sentence. To be abandoned as an early human meant to starve, freeze, or face the wolves and tigers alone, whichever came first. Unsurprisingly, you and I still find it hard to take. Because social bonds are so necessary to our survival, all our systems evolved to recoil from rejection. We don't just experience it in terms of mental, emotional, and psychological strife— though heaven knows we experience it in those ways fully enough—but as physical pain.

In fact, researchers have found that OTC drugs such as Tylenol can help to lessen this pain, as though being told to get out of your parents' house were the same thing as a migraine or a strained hamstring. So profoundly does rejection affect us, so greatly do we fear it, that we even experience it *secondhand*—we can feel rejected vicariously. This is why you can't look away from all those "try not to cringe" compilations on YouTube, and why reading Poe's abject teenage pleas makes you want to clap his *Collected Letters* shut, toss the book out the window, and go swimming in a fishbowl of Chablis.

Our deep dread of rejection also accounts for why, according to numerous surveys, public speaking ranks as people's number-one fear, ahead of snakes, spiders, heights, premature burial, and the Spanish Inquisition. Even now you may feel the clammy, phantom wood of some distant lectern beneath your palms as the senseless drivel pours, uncontrollably, from your gullet. Nothing focuses the mind like that kind of self-consciousness so awful, so severe you almost want to *laugh at yourself* alongside those laughing at you.

Yet all of us will face rejection at some point. No one is exempt, which makes it all the more important that you understand how to have the right response—that, no matter your age or exact situation, you harness the gut-searing motivation that rejection can provide you, and make an ardent resolution like Poe himself made. "If you determine to abandon me," he ranted to Allan in another letter later that year, "I will be doubly ambitious, & the world shall hear of the son whom you have thought unworthy of your notice."

Give up? Hell no. At this key turning point, Poe *doubled down on his ambitions*, because if he didn't, then everything Allan believed about him—that he was an idler, a loser, good-for-nothing—would be true. But you don't have to mirror Poe's exact playbook, which involved hopping a ship from Richmond to Boston, Massachusetts, assuming an alias, and, while starving and struggling to find work, paying out of his own pocket to publish his first book of poems, *Tamerlane*.* You just need to nail the larger moves, outlined below.

Step 1. Decide on revenge-via-success

Revenge, in this age of AR-15s, may strike a scary note. What we speak of here is nothing so cheap and cowardly, but what Poe himself sought: revenge-via-success (i.e., *showing them all*). Whether you are reacting to a rejection by your parents, by a would-be prom date, by your first-choice college or grad school, or if you've been fired from a job or are experiencing a surprise divorce, now is the moment to become "doubly ambitious" and tackle the huge task of *forcing the world to care about you, at last*. It's time to make your mark, to prove to your foster father and all the other dim bulbs in your hometown that you are the person you know yourself to be. Whatever you'd planned to do with your life before, *expand the plan*. Make your mission grander, more epic, so that an entire lifetime may be required to fulfill it.

This step, counterintuitively, is more about you and your self-respect than it is anything external. Revenge-via-success is something you do for you, a form of self-care.

You're gifting yourself a huge sense of purpose at a moment when you might otherwise be floundering, rudderless. So screw your heart up

---

* The alias Poe used was Henri Le Rennet. Nicely glamorous and foreign, no?

tight. Suck in your breath. Swear to yourself that one day they—whoever "they" are—will *rue the day* they doubted you. Even if, like a good lapsed Catholic, you long to forgive and you wish good things for everyone no matter what they've done to you, be sure you nurse a little desire for revenge as well. It'll keep you warm at night in your single bed at the hostel, in your cramped seat on the Bolt Bus, and during your overnight shift in the glass cage at the bodega. Poe would want you to, and, frankly, you're going to need it.

Step 2. Change addresses in a big way

Some folks stay where they are and try to mend the hurt. Don't. Go! Leave! Embrace the impulse to run. The place where you've been rejected has become a psychic prison, and putting it in your rearview is as much as a spiritual step as a physical one—marking the beginning of your mythic antihero's journey. The anthropologist Joseph Campbell identified such decisive departure as the outset of your unique, glorious destiny, a literal call to adventure. "The familiar life horizon has been outgrown," Campbell wrote, "the old concepts, ideals, and emotional patterns no longer fit; the time for the passing of the threshold is at hand."

Granted, you may think you can't afford to pass the threshold. Of course you can't. Few of us can. Do it anyway. Action beats planning. Just pull up stakes, whether that means moving to the nearest city from your rural county—ah, the bright lights of Topeka!—or to an actual big city on the coast, where every day you have to choose between rent and lunch. It hardly matters where. Fail to remove yourself from the scene of rejection

and you'll miss one of life's great chances.* You may be broke, yet a new world awaits you. What notions of spectacular vindication will you nourish? Your life is now either (a) spinning out of control or (b) taking a turn wilder and weirder than you ever deemed possible.

Think of those who've come before you and take heart. Generations of theater kids, queer kids, artists, intellectuals, freaks, and dissidents of all

---

* Sometimes our life circumstances include custody battles, court dates, and/or ankle bracelets, and we cannot move. In this case, opt for mental departure. Draw a firm mental line behind you, like you're not going back—back to that place, that job, that relationship, self, life, et cetera.

stripes have all left their hometowns for bigger arenas. Buddha did it, so did Jesus. Poe too. Why not you? Crucially, such a move will also free you to exaggerate how well you're doing in the new location—perhaps even to convince some indifferent ex that you're in an exciting new relationship when you are, uh, not. Lock down all the wins, friend—real or, you know, invented. You're in charge of your own narrative now, and only *you* get to decide what's fake news.

Poe tip #5: Rejected? Humiliated? Adopt a fake name and flee town, ideally under cover of night. Return when, and *only* when, you're rich, famous, and successful—or able to convincingly present yourself as such.

And don't worry. The rest of the Poe-gram will show you how to make all those "I'm doing great, just GREAT" lies actually come true.

The Antihero's Journey

Use the handy chart below to measure your progress against Poe's. Where are you on your antihero's journey right now? Wherever that may be, just be sure you're on the *wrong* track. Remember—it's all a matter of perspective.

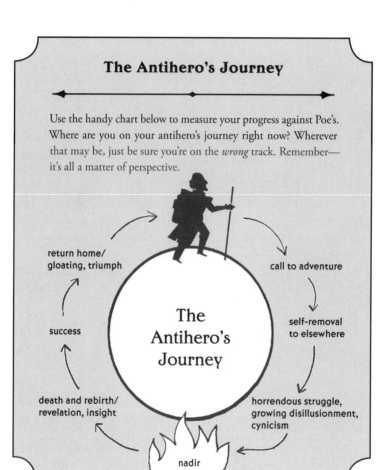

return home/
gloating, triumph

call to adventure

The
Antihero's
Journey

success

self-removal
to elsewhere

death and rebirth/
revelation, insight

horrendous struggle,
growing disillusionment,
cynicism

nadir

PART 2

Career and Poe-sonal Finance

If you've ever stared up at the ladder of success from its bottommost rung, wondering if your big break will ever come, then you know Poe's mood in 1827. There's the work you ache to do. Then there's the work you *have* to do to survive. Read on to discover Poe's professional and financial struggles, and grasp how you, too, can:

➤ Pivot from youthful idealism to crass commercialism

➤ Get pre-fired—that is, *hired*

➤ Triumph (sort of!) in hand-to-hand professional combat

Plus, peep Poe's tips for fudging your résumé, inflating your workplace contributions, and making the most of your doomed entrepreneurial dreams.

Why Selling Out Is Your First Step to Success

Ugh. Sorry, sweetheart. As sexy as you are in your early twenties, your life is tending toward a comedown, a great big smacking confrontation with reality. Poe's experience was no different. He fell hard down the social scale when he left his foster father's house, and he felt it.

From a mansion with its own mirrored ballroom in Richmond, Poe was reduced to grim boardinghouses in Boston—to scrambling just for his next meal. He nursed hopes, at first, of working as a clerk or a journalist, maybe even trying his hand at acting, but hunger and poverty soon forced a more practical choice. In May of 1827, Poe joined the US Army under yet another fake name.* What followed was a series of swampy, mosquito-infested posts. Endless drills and orders. Three hots, a barracks cot—only this and nothing more.

When, in early 1829, the news came that his foster mother had fallen ill, Poe couldn't reach Richmond in time. He didn't arrive home until the day after she died, didn't get the chance to say goodbye. The silver lining, however faint, was this: in their shared grief, he and John Allan reconciled. Back in his foster father's good graces, Poe could dream again.

---

* Edgar A. Perry. Not nearly as melodious as "Henri Le Rennet," but probably easier to remember. With fake names, it's always a balance.

He quickly hatched a plan to realize his grand ambitions after all. If John Allan would only help him win an appointment to the service academy at West Point, then he could rise to become a commissioned officer, and all his problems might be solved at once. He could gain financial independence and reclaim the social status he craved. Most importantly, he'd get the leisure time to focus on his poetry, and become, at last, the world famous genius-scholar-writer of his dreams.

"At my time of life there is much in being *before the eye of the world*," he gushed to John Allan in a letter, unwisely. "If only noticed I can easily cut out a path to reputation."

John Allan proved willing enough to help, at least with the first part of Poe's scheme. Poe going to West Point meant Poe staying out of Richmond, which John Allan hardly minded. He was less keen on the part of the plan that would have him underwriting Poe's publishing projects. Though Poe had found a press willing to put out an expansion of his earlier *Tamerlane*, tricked out with some new material, John Allan would need to make good any losses the press might incur, up to $100, or about $3,000 today. This Allan declined to do, replying to the request by "strongly censuring" Poe's conduct.

Once again, relations cooled right off, before downright freezing and cracking in two. In the 1830s equivalent of somebody screenshotting your angry text and sending it to the *subject* of that text, a resentful army acquaintance forwarded John Allan a letter in which Poe had described him, *Allan*, as a drunk ("not very often sober" in Poe's exact phrasing).*

---

* Granted, the guy had his reasons for forwarding the letter: he'd taken Poe's place in the army and Poe still owed him money.

Poe might as well have fired one of his fancy army cannons: whatever esteem or good vibes might've still existed between the two was blown to smithereens.

Poe's experience of West Point didn't solve anything. Against all odds, the nation's most elite military academy turned out to be . . . a military academy. A highly regimented service institution. Not the kind of place that'd let you lie around dreaming up epics and perfecting your couplets. Poe responded by racking up enough demerits to earn himself a court-martial, in 1831. The military was no place for a poor man like him, he'd decided, not now that John Allan had unfriended him on Venmo. *Again.*

Eventually, Poe drifted down to Baltimore. He'd kept up contact with his biological father's side of the family, and now he moved into a cramped house with his grandmother, aunt, cousin, and brother. None of these relatives had two dimes to rub together, and neither did Poe. He was twenty-two years old, broke, miserable, and in some ways even worse off than before.[*]

If all this seems like a welter of flailing and grasping at straws, ending in no great triumph—more like the opposite of triumph, a years-long struggle to land somewhere *worse* than where you started from—well, it was. But we need not despair. Poe's brutal twentysomething comedown served him *incredibly* well, in the same way that yours may serve you. Over the next few months and years, Poe came to the critical realization

---

[*] Poe actually managed to publish two more books of poetry about this time, even without John Allan's help. Still, they did almost nothing to improve his prospects. The eye of the world was looking everywhere else.

that no one was going to finance his doing exactly what he wanted to do, and he made a choice. If no one would fork out for his poetry, then he'd write stories: The turned-up-to-eleven kind about shipwrecks, ghosts, hauntings, toothless corpses, and old wives coming back from the dead only to murder new wives. Super goth stuff. Uber commercial.

This was not his dream. Poe scoffed at the spine-tinglers even as he churned them out, oblivious to the fact that his brazen sell-out would still be winning him readers almost two hundred years later. All he knew at the time was that magazines and newspapers would pay for such material, and so he could start to eke out a living as a freelance writer (just see the next lesson on page 53).

Unemployable twenty-something, meet career.

This is the exact problem most of us are trying to solve at twenty-three, twenty-four, and twenty-five—and some of us are still trying to solve at thirty-five, fifty-five, and beyond. Figuring out how to make a living is one of life's greatest challenges. Most of us suffer at least a few years of spinning out, taking up paths and abandoning them, begging our loved ones for a place to stay and maybe a co-signature on a loan (can you *hear* my dad sighing?), before we figure out a way to earn steady cash. Hell. Cash, period.

Why? Because our first-choice professions aren't always feasible. We grow up dreaming of becoming poets, comedians, film directors, actors, musicians, models, chefs, scholars, or one of those people whose job is to post about luxury hotels on Instagram. We crave prestige, respect, and expense accounts. We would really prefer that our wealthy foster fathers finance our lifestyle fantasies, and that we never have to dirty our hands, compromise our visions, or scrape and bow to the demands of the marketplace. Which is odd given what a *tremendous advantage* it is to learn to think in terms of what will sell. And yet it's understandable, too. Financial concerns tend not to come at us like buoys bobbing along on the surface of a calm ocean. Instead, they present as giant, sucking whirlpools—a torrent of cold water chilling the body, plus the very real chance of total personal annihilation. The truths we discover about money and economics we mostly discover against our will.

You might choose to be more proactive. Say there's a field you're desperate to break into. Maybe it's an artistic field like literature or music, or an art-adjacent field such as fashion, design, food, sports, or live events. Whatever it is, your first move is to understand how individuals and whole companies in that field make money (i.e., what the underlying economic picture looks like). This will give you the best possible sense of where the opportunities lie—who the producers are, who the consumers are, where supply meets demand.

Now, that might sound elementary as hell, like Business 101, yet many of us never take that class, expecting it to be a snooze, when nothing could be further from the truth. Developing economic insight is to develop insight, period. All the world's a stage—all the world's a marketplace, too. As the economist and blogger Tyler Cowen has pointed out, economics is at heart a branch of anthropology, or the study of human behavior across cultures and through time. Paying attention to the ebb and flow of the market, tracking cash flows as they slosh through a system, allows you to tap into one of the most important sources of information there is. You learn to bird-dog incentives and to analyze people's motives beyond what they *say* their motives are, making you a more skillful negotiator, better able to evaluate situations and foresee future developments. You gain the sophistication to see past glib slogans and to identify the flaws in other people's thinking (not to mention their marketing plans), as well as your own.

Chances are that you will also get better at your work, whatever your work happens to be. Selling out made Poe a *better writer*, not just a more successful one. He found a positive-feedback loop: the longer he went on writing commercial pieces, the more his genius grew, until he was composing the masterpieces of his mature career, from "The Tell-Tale Heart" to "The Cask of Amontillado," to crowd-pleasing poems like "Annabel Lee." In his thirties, he would go so far as to boast that he wrote "The Gold-Bug" and "The Raven" to achieve those high-minded artistic goals, money and fame.

The market Poe focused on was magazine publishing, which in his day, on the back of a tech breakthrough, was seeing a spike of explosive growth akin to the early days of the internet. Your market will be different. The lesson still holds. You cannot excel in a field if you can't grasp it on its most basic level, if you don't understand the underlying *why* and *how*. Neither can you locate a career or a unique position for yourself in the marketplace, like Poe did with his intellectually and psychologically souped-up goth stories. So often that it's more the rule than the exception, there lies a vast ocean between what people say they want (searing indie dramas, steamed vegetables) and what they truly want (TikTok, Kardashians, waffle fries). As often, the sheer savviest move you can make is simply *lowering your standards*, choosing to work in a field that's adjacent to your dream field, perhaps slightly down-market from what you originally conceived. Your greatest opportunities may well exist in an arena that all your friends regard as crass, gross, dumb, disappointing, too low to go.

Maybe this means you try an un-trendy city, an un-cool job, a lesser platform, something more mainstream than hip or cutting-edge. Just don't let anyone else make you feel guilty for attempting to earn a living, and adjusting to the marketplace so as to be able to pay Sallie Mae, keep your cat in Fancy Feast, and get your name out there. Don't be ashamed of *surviving*.

The best-case scenario? Forced to earn a damn living, you develop a wide-ranging understanding of your field. You become both a practitioner and a theoretician, an ideas man, woman, person. You develop an intuitive grasp of workable notions and a set of instincts that you can continue to hone for the rest of your career. Even Poe, with his unwieldy, overloaded wheelbarrow of an ego, his intermittent mental health, and his weakness for the sauce, managed to reach an audience and even to *get a job* every now and again.

So can you.

Poe tip #6: Sell out as soon as possible, and when in doubt, look down-market for opportunity.

A Descent into the Mainstream

In Poe's 1841 short story "A Descent into the Maelström," a fisherman is sucked into a ferocious whirlpool, but survives by clinging to a barrel. Consider this a metaphor for your entry into the working world. You can't avoid the whirlpool, and it *is* going to suck, but you must survive somehow. Meditate upon the following commercial versions of your cherished creative dreams and get inspired to move down-market. Then fill in the blank.

Writing ➔ Journalism (see below)

Journalism ➔ Advertising; marketing

Drawing, painting, visual art ➔ Hock logos on Fiverr; graphic and web design

Dance ➔ Exotic dance

Comedy ➔ Clown at children's birthday parties; drive an Uber

Cuisine ➔ Manage an Olive Garden; shop for Instacart

Screenwriting, acting ➔ Marry some big-time producer

Academia ➔ Teach high school

_____ ➔ _____
(your dream)   (its practical incarnation)

Fast-Talking Your Way into a "Real" Job

In 1833, at age twenty-four, Edgar Allan Poe won first prize in a Baltimore short-story contest, pocketing the $50 prize (about $1,500 today). This was his first big break. He not only took home the laurels, but he found a market for his freelance work and met a new circle of elite people whom he could now beg and *beg* for favors. Not least among these was John Pendleton Kennedy, a writer and politician about fifteen years his senior, who had served as one of the contest judges.

Soon after they met, Poe's pleading letters began arriving at Kennedy's home. Poe hoped Kennedy would help him find a publisher for his short stories, and though he *very* much wanted to accept Kennedy's dinner invitation, he had to decline "for reasons of the most humiliating nature in my personal appearance." That is, he didn't have the proper clothes. Maybe he could borrow $20 (about $600) to get some? No need to answer now. He'd drop by tomorrow to pick up the cash.

In Poe's defense, he *was* desperate. Rumors suggest he may have been day-laboring at a brickyard during this time, though the established facts are bleak enough. John Allan died in early 1834, yet left Poe nothing of his vast estate. At the same time, even as Poe's freelance career grew, the income from his magazine and newspaper contributions was too spotty to support him—as any freelancer waiting vainly for a check can appreciate. Kennedy understood Poe's financial dilemma and encouraged Poe to tilt even further away from his artistic ideals, drudging instead "upon whatever may make money." He also saw that what Poe needed most of all was a salaried position, or as it's known today, a "real" job. So, in 1835, he put Poe in touch with his friend T. W. White, who'd recently launched a magazine called the *Southern Literary Messenger*.

Poe's letters now turned in the direction of White's Richmond office, except their tone changed in a crucial, downright shrewd way. "I beg you to believe that I have no intention of giving you *advice*," he breezed to White, "being fully confident that, upon consideration, you will agree with me." The entire history of the magazine industry—an industry in which Poe implied he was an expert—showed that good taste didn't matter one whit. Only by ignoring such boring conventions, Poe argued, could a magazine succeed. Forget subtlety, refinement, tact. Better to fill your pages with the fearful and the horrible, grabbing readers by the throat. Or, as modern editors advise: "If it bleeds, it leads."

Bowled over by this bluster, White was convinced of Poe's savvy. Though he had *really* been hoping to make a different editorial hire, after his desired candidate turned down his offer of $800 a year, he offered the position to Poe at a much lower salary: $10 a week, or $520 a year. Adjusted for inflation, that just about equals today's federal minimum wage of $7.25 an hour if you're working full time. Poe's room and board alone would consume almost half his earnings, but he could write for the *Messenger* on top of his many other tasks, earning a few dollars more. The gig would be two parts grudging secretarial nightmare, one part dream job. Nevertheless, he'd made it. He sprinted down to Richmond, his old hometown, to assume his duties.

Leaps don't come much bigger than the one from broke-ass to employed. Even if you've managed to land some freelance work, or the odd unpaid internship, the chasm remains vast. Getting your first real job is always a feat. It's much the same if you're trying to switch fields in midcareer—you've got to convince some poor, unsuspecting dope that you're bright-eyed, bushy-tailed, eager to join the team, and, above all, *qualified* when what you actually feel is only a clammy, gnawing sense of poverty and insecurity, like, *Oh god pick me because my Verizon bill. Also I haven't seen a dentist in eight years.* The situation is all the more difficult because, just like Poe, you confront the age-old catch-22: you can't get an entry-level job without experience, and you need an entry-level job to gain that experience.

Poe's workaround highlights the potential upside in (a) shamelessly working your connections in order to get an interview at all, and (b) feigning confidence and expertise, as if you've already worked a million such jobs. The moral? Always act like you've been here before, no matter how desperate you may be. No one wants to hire the girl with sweaty palms, or the red-faced guy offering to sweep the floors. No one even wants to make *eye contact* with that person. Groveling is almost never a good look. You have to even the playing field, for your own sake and theirs. And the way to accomplish this is by mastering the larger psychological game.

The good news is, if you followed the previous lesson (see page 44), then you have already gained sales experience of a kind. You've sold your ideals in the marketplace, exchanging them for a new attitude of "Who cares about quality, let's talk marketing," plus a new appreciation for supply and demand. Building on this experience and putting these principles into action is your next step.

Psychologists use the term "theory of mind" to explain our understanding that other people—just like ourselves—have needs, wants, thoughts, and problems of their own (the needy bastards). So, too, does this hiring manager whom you're trying to convince to give you a chance. The key is to think through their desires and what problems they're attempting to solve. Recall how, when writing that bold letter to White, Poe didn't talk about his own goals. He did not—as when he first began submitting freelance work to magazines—come right out and say, "I am poor." Instead, Poe focused on White's goals. He guessed that White wanted readers for his magazine, so he spoke to how White might attract readers. And to boost his own credibility, he spoke of the magazine industry as a whole, its past and future.

In doing so, Poe transformed his own weaknesses into strengths. Up to this point, of course, he'd never worked as an editor before. He had patchy, intermittent freelance experience—and only a few years' worth of that. Yet he presented this experience not as fitful but as broad, wide-ranging, insightful. You can do the same with your own disparate bits of classwork, freelance work, previous part-time jobs, and/or internships. You also have a great advantage over Poe in that he didn't have access to Google or Wikipedia, so he couldn't panic-search "history of the magazine industry" or "key trends in magazine publishing" before he sat down to compose that quasi-cover letter. If he could have presented the thoughts of some random Wikipedia contributor as his own, well, the history of his career suggests he might have. He didn't just present himself as an authority on magazines when talking to White—he cribbed from encyclopedias and other works throughout his life.

As the scholar Terence Whalen dryly noted of our man Edgar: "At one time or another during his career, he claimed expertise in law, phrenology, landscape gardening, navigation, geology, Hebrew, French, Greek, Latin, cryptography, painting, road-building, natural history, ancient history, aeronautics, political economy, conchology, corkscrews, mathematics, astronomy, Baconian science, religion, music, field sports, and the philosophy of furniture."

What guts, what chutzpah. What an instructive example for the rest of us.

Of course, you may be too nervous to feign such knowledge, because you fear the person on the other end of your application knows so much more about their industry than you do. This is a common misconception, easy to fall prey to if you haven't spent much time in corporate offices. Do not let it deter you. The truth is that everyone is incompetent, management most of all. This is not mere speculation, but long-established, *well*-established management theory. *The Peter Principle*, a management manifesto first published in 1969, argued that, in organizations, individuals rise to their "level of incompetence."* Thus, anyone in a position to hire you is probably unqualified to do so.

The great 1980s–90s comic *Dilbert* built on this idea, portraying managers as actively, dangerously harmful to *the organizations they are empowered to lead*. The now-classic 1999 film *Office Space* cannily suggested that laziness and a disregard for authority might turn out to be the best qualifications for promotion to the upper ranks. Even more recently, the blogger Venkatesh Rao released *The Gervais Principle*, arguing that middle management in particular is put into place to take the blame for and cover up the maneuverings of the checked-out sociopaths at the top of the organizational pyramid. In other words, that hiring manager you're meeting with? They probably can't do their job. They're just there to cover for even *more* senior people who can't, or won't, do *their* jobs.

Bearing these ideas in mind, you're better able to read the person you're interviewing with, and hopefully negotiating with. They likely

---

* I know this having just consulted the Wikipedia entry. See how I'm eating Poe's cooking, too?

know even less about the position than you do, but you can never acknowledge or allude to that fact. Tempted though you may be, you must not come out and act superior. Remember that incompetent people are *more* apt to be touchy and vain than competent people, not less. Instead, gently, gracefully take for granted your interviewer's grasp of industry history and truisms, just as Poe did in his letter to White. Again: "I beg you to believe that I have no intention of giving you *advice*, being fully confident that, upon consideration, you will agree with me." That's some first-class inspirational schmoozing. Feel free to steal the line. Poe would if he were you.

Poe tip #7: Always act like you've been here before. Making grand claims about industries you're not really familiar with is a great way to seem savvy and in-the-know.

Once you've locked down a real job (and most importantly, a real salary), you can begin inventing even more experience, transforming duties like "answered the phone" into "drove revenue by liaising with clients from initial contact to final point of sale." Or whatever. You will also find your-self—at last—initiated into The Great Secret of Working Life, which is that the only thing worse than not having a job is having one. (Welcome, friend! Join the rest of us for happy hour?) Poe discovered the Secret, too, in the fullness of time. He would soon come to resent his editorship, White, the *Messenger*, all of it, and he'd be angling for some other, slightly less horrible, ill-paid and soul-killing job. May you be so lucky.

Poe's 10 Best Tips for Getting Ahead in the Workplace Once You've Gotten Your Foot in the Door*

←————————•————————→

---

* Just kidding. He had none. He was let go from the *Messenger* inside of two years, as you're about to see.

LESSON #8

What Color Is Your Seashell Scam?

So long as your mind is ready to receive it, Poe is now prepared to dispense a great and neglected lesson—what you might call his #1 Money Secret. It begins with the epic economic crisis that erupted almost as soon as he left his first real job.

"Left" is the polite word. Less than two years in, Poe and White had seen just about enough of each other. They'd quarreled about Poe's overbearing editorial style, his tendency to write scathing reviews, and about his drinking. "No man is safe who drinks before breakfast!" White warned Poe, not unreasonably. "No man can do so, and attend to business properly."* Plus, Poe had itchy feet. At first delighted by the job, he'd come to see how "the drudgery was excessive, the salary was contemptible," and he longed to move on to bigger, better things. So, in early 1837, he upped stakes and moved to New York, convinced he had a good lead on a fancier job, and full of confidence that, in a larger city, he could carve out a flashier reputation.

It would soon become clear what a *terrible* moment he'd chosen to trade up. New York—and the rest of the United States—was, within months,

---

* Sadly, we have no record of Poe's response. But I imagine something along the lines of *How dare you question my morning quart!*

struck by the worst financial crisis in its history, unsurpassed until the Great Depression almost a century later. In the Panic of 1837, banks failed, real estate prices plummeted, and tens of thousands of people lost their livelihoods. Poe's New York job never materialized, and he could hardly find any freelance work, either.

On top of this, he now had a family to support, with his wife and mother-in-law living under his roof, or lack of one (more on Poe's marriage later). The family spent a hungry, hardscrabble year trying to make it in Manhattan before fleeing to Philadelphia, seeking greener pastures. It did no good. Poe still couldn't find a job. Simply paying the rent required "the most painful sacrifices," including, it seems, borrowing money from neighbors. At times, they had nothing to eat for weeks on end but bread and molasses.

Poe needed money like a man dying of thirst needs a Big Gulp. Hoping to score some quick cash, he speed-wrote a novel he hoped might become a commercial blockbuster: *The Narrative of Arthur Gordon Pym of Nantucket*, a sea-faring adventure story stuffed to the gills with stunning developments, shocking twists, and a light, refreshing spritz of cannibalism. It was published in 1838 by Harper & Brothers, then one of the largest and most powerful media companies in the country. Despite the advantageous printing, the reviews were mixed, the public reception lukewarm. His pay amounted to just a few copies *of his own book*, and his money problems only persisted. Poe's next move put his desperation on full display. He got involved in a convoluted literary scam involving, of all things, conchology, or the study of mollusk seashells.

His friend Thomas Wyatt had written a conchology manual—creatively titled *Manual of Conchology*—which Harper & Brothers had put out in

a swank, illustrated edition. It sold well at a high price point, and the firm was not keen to undercut such a moneymaker. Wyatt, however, yearned to capture more of the market. In 1839, he arranged for Poe to be paid $50 to put his name on a cheap, essentially plagiarized version, *The Conchologist's First Book*, that Wyatt could shill at his lectures for $1.50 a copy (while, presumably, keeping some of the profits). All Poe had to do was add a new introduction and some other editorial window dressing, and, of course, allow his name to be used. Poe took the deal and pocketed the money, but when the word got out, his reputation suffered—perhaps most of all with Harper & Brothers, who refused to work with him for years afterward. The sea salt in the wound? Poe's bogus seashell manual outsold not just *Pym*, but all his previous books, too. It would become the only one of "his" books to go into a second printing during his lifetime.

Generations of commentators have sneered at this episode, as if Poe both enjoyed a smorgasbord of options at the time and lacked the moral sense to pursue the better ones. In the 1870s, a Harvard professor explained Poe's role in the scheme by saying he'd been selected as an "irresponsible person whom it would be idle to sue for damages," nothing more than a handy, penniless scapegoat. In 1992, the Poe biographer Jeffrey Meyers upped the ante, calling Poe "perfectly irresponsible."

You too might've assumed, until now, that Poe's well-known financial problems were all his fault, and that his hackwork was necessary because he lacked principles and beer money. But Poe didn't cause the economic crisis that lasted almost the entire span of his professional life. The Panic of 1837 and its aftereffects lingered well into the mid-1840s. In the words of historian Sydney Ahlstrom, it "darkened the dream" of even the most optimistic members of Poe's generation.

Amid this crisis, Poe glimpsed more of the realities of his dream industry, too. In his mind the exciting world of magazines had begun to resemble a "prison-house," with good reason. No matter his skill and gutsiness in adapting to the marketplace, the larger financial and legal system of the day made it extraordinarily difficult to monetize his output. Worst of all was the lack of an international copyright law, which meant that his work could be pirated abroad, and that the American market, in which he naturally hoped to find his greatest success, was saturated by "free" material similarly pirated from Europe. As the scholar Sandra Tomc pointed out, all this had the effect of driving down rates for American authors' work, including stories, poems, novels, essays—every genre in which Poe worked. Why would publishers fork out for original material when they could grab proven winners from overseas at no expense? Why would they pay any local writer so much as a handful of sticky couch change when they didn't have to?

The pissant sums Poe earned for the brilliant stories he published during this period look a whole lot better once you understand what he was up against—you realize the amazing thing is that he managed to make *any* money at all with his creative work. His scraping together even a threadbare living begins to look like triumph, not failure. You realize as well why he sometimes participated in the travesty. Glance at the table following, and you'll see that the bogus seashell manual alone brought in more money than "Ligeia," "The Masque of the Red Death," and "The Man of the Crowd" *combined*—all of which now rank among his greatest-ever works. During these hard-pressed years, begging neighbors and distant family also appears to have brought Poe more cash than all but a few of his masterpieces.

TITLE	YEAR PUBLISHED	ORIGINAL PAYMENT	APPROX. AMOUNT IN 2020 DOLLARS
"Ligeia"	1838	$10	$279
The Conchologist's First Book	1839	$50	$1,397
"The Haunted Palace"	1839	$5	$139
"The Fall of the House of Usher"	1839	$24	$671
"The Man of the Crowd"	1840	$16	$478
"The Masque of the Red Death"	1842	$12	$380
"The Pit and the Pendulum"	1842	$38	$1,204
"The Tell-Tale Heart"	1843	$10	$351
"The Black Cat"	1843	$20	$702
"The Gold-Bug"	1843	$100	$3,512
"The Raven"	1845	$9	$307
"The Cask of Amontillado"	1846	$15	$506
"Ulalume"	1847	$20	$634
"Annabel Lee"	1849	$10	$337

If you boiled the financial principle down to a formula, it would look like this:

Brilliant creative work < petty scams + scrounging

Did Poe love this reality? Was it what he would have chosen to be the logic of his economic universe? No. Naturally, there's a lesson in this for you, though I realize it all may seem like so much dusty history. Thankfully, sudden, horrific financial crises that mangle our lives without our consent are a thing of the past, hahahahaha. *Sob.*

You are going to live through periods of economic malaise. You may have already, depending on your age, so maybe you know a little bit about what it means to face the kinds of dilemmas Poe faced, and to be forced to make similar trade-offs between what you believe in and what you have to do just to survive. More than a few of us have had to ask our nearest and dearest for a loan, lest we resort to the payday loan people or GoFundMe, *again.*

Considering that we also live in an age in which many of us create content and data for giant tech companies all day long for free, you probably realize that notions of intellectual property and who-owns-what can seem boring at first glance, yet mean the difference between feasting on steak and choking down bread and molasses. It remains true in our day, to boot, that creatives of all stripes tend to be among those hardest hit by financial pullbacks—they're the "last hired, first fired" of the entire culture because such work is often viewed as a luxury good or, worse still, an abundant natural resource that no one should have to pay for.

You rarely hear about such hard realities in books about personal finance. The classics of the genre tend to emphasize only the "personal" aspect of finance—namely, your need to demonstrate determination, resilience, and fortitude. The problem is not how you may have been set up to fail—no, it's all in your mindset. In Napoleon Hill's *Think and Grow Rich*, and again in Robert Kiyosaki's *Rich Dad, Poor Dad*, you're informed that financial success is primarily a matter of unwavering self-belief. Unless you *believe* you can get rich, or are actively able to envision yourself as rich already, you're lost. Just another sad-sack loser dialing the unemployment office.

Such delusions can be useful, and here in the Poe-verse we should have no beef with megalomaniacal personal visions. At the same time, Poe's experience makes clear that the opposite is also true. You can feel a deep sense of purpose, be in relentless pursuit of your goals, have a burning desire for greatness *and* cash, yet remain poor. You can think and grow broke. Write and grow broker. You can have a rich (foster) dad and a poor (biological) dad, like Poe, and still end up screwed. Brilliance, imagination, and mental ingenuity can go unrewarded, while hackwork and scams can get you through the inevitable lean times. Let your future biographers sneer. You gotta do what you gotta do. Don't you think that if it truly were possible to merely *think* your way to amazing wealth, if the "law of attraction" really worked—per Rhonda Byrne's *The Secret* and all those other hokey books—there would be many more millionaires, and far fewer Americans just trying to pay the damn rent?

Poe tip #8: Scams are far more reliable moneymakers than dreams (or dreams within dreams). When unsuccessful financially, feel free to blame vast socioeconomic forces beyond your control.

Sure, none of this is what you'd call positive news. More like Poe-sitive news, in keeping with everything else you've learned thus far about the adult world. Call it a dark awakening—one that marks a graduation to the more advanced phase of your career. You're developing a sense of the landscape as it really is, a considered view of how the world actually operates versus how it purports to operate. And there's even some upside. Understanding that your financial failure is not necessarily your fault has a way of taking the pressure off.

When your moonshot projects—selling that screenplay, inventing that better mousetrap, launching that start-up or app—fail to generate vast riches through which you can swim like Scrooge McDuck, feel free to blame the system instead. You're probably correct! The lack of cash and recognition you're feeling now is no barrier whatsoever to your future recognition as a world-changing genius. Neither is cadging money or doing the odd bit of hackwork that you're not proud of. Period. End of story. Forget your parachute—what color is your seashell scam?

How to Conduct Yourself in a Feud

Whether or not you're as gifted as Poe in torpedoing your interpersonal relationships, it is inevitable that, at some point in your career, you will have a giant idiot for a boss—someone whom you can't stand, and who can't stand you.

When in 1839 William Evans Burton offered Poe a job, you have to think Poe was relieved. His income for much of the previous two years had averaged just 16 cents a day ($4 in today's money), and this to support a household of three. Even so, Burton's offer letter was a veritable thicket of red flags, a red-flag forest composed of red-flag trees.

Burton owned and published *The Gentleman's Magazine*, a voluminous *GQ*-like rag dedicated to manly pursuits like hunting and nationalism, but he was also an actor who often traveled outside Philadelphia to perform. What he needed, he said, was an assistant who could help him make sure the magazine ran to schedule. The job would be very simple—so simple it probably wouldn't take up very much of Poe's time at all. "Two hours per day, except occasionally, will, I believe, be sufficient for all required," he told Poe. Unfortunately, "expenses of the Magazine are already woefully heavy," so Burton couldn't offer much compensation, not while "competition is high" and "my contributors cost me something handsome." Given these regrettable conditions, would Poe be willing to accept "ten dollars per week for the remaining portion of the year?"

Ten dollars per week was, of course, the same crappy, "contemptible" salary Poe had been offered by the *Messenger*, four years earlier. He just didn't have any room to bargain, much less to turn the job down. Any paycheck is better than no paycheck, and it all might have worked out fine if Burton's description of the hours had been accurate. Which—surprise, surprise—it was not. Once he got started, Poe found he was often stuck running the entire show himself. To hear him tell it, his job duties included corresponding with contributors; selecting, revising, and preparing manuscripts; writing reviews as well as some articles (about eleven pages per month in his estimation); *and* supervising the magazine's printing. Meanwhile Burton treated him not like an equal but like an underling.

Never mind how much he needed the job, needed the money. Poe's response to this treatment was characteristic, i.e., embittered, self-defeating, and *instructive*. Learning in the spring of 1840 that Burton planned to sell the magazine, Poe decided to launch his own magazine—a direct competitor. The two exchanged angry letters, and Poe found himself canned all over again.

We know this in part because Poe kept a draft of the letter he wrote Burton after the relationship turned briny, and it makes for an excellent crib sheet for when your *own* workplace relations erupt. Writing some of his best fiction at the time, the thirty-one-year-old Poe was near the apex of his rhetorical powers, too. Feast your eyes, my friend, on these two morsels.

PART 1.

In the first place—your attempts to bully me excite in my mind scarcely any other sentiment than mirth. When you address me again preserve if you can, the dignity of a gentleman. If by accident you have taken it into your head that I am to be insulted with impunity I can only assume that you are an ass. This one point being distinctly understood I shall feel myself more at liberty to be explicit. As for the rest, you do me gross injustice; and you know it. As usual you have wrought yourself into a passion with me on account of some imaginary wrong; for no real injury, or attempt at injury, have you ever received at my hands. As I live, I am utterly unable to say why you are angry, or what true grounds of complaint you have against me. You are a man of impulses; have made yourself, in consequence, some enemies; have been in many respects ill treated by those whom you had looked upon as friends—and these things have rendered you suspicious.

PART 2.

You first "enforced", as you say, a deduction of salary: giving me to understand thereby that you thought of parting company— You next spoke disrespectfully of me behind my back—this as an habitual thing—to those whom you supposed your friends, and who punctually retailed me, as a matter of course, every ill-natured word which you uttered.

What can we learn? Plenty. Almost two hundred years have passed since these two men began slapping each other about the face with indignant accusations and counteraccusations, yet human nature remains the same. We are all still just jumped-up territorial creatures who, having shared a watercooler too long, leap into battle over the pettiest of shit. You need not be ashamed of your outsized reaction or your tendency to hold grudges. If you read the first section of this book, you already *know* these are your best qualities, how you've gotten this far.

And the workplace—because it is the natural habitat of petty tyrants, as well as craven, useless bottom-feeders and the kind of three-eyed cretins who gleefully waste their lives undermining others via their positions in HR—can only bring these qualities of yours even further to the fore. Spending just a few months inside such a place may be all that's necessary. You may have discovered a nemesis without even trying, and may now find yourself battling some boss or coworker or client while, like Poe, struggling to get in your last digs and poison darts before the giant hook comes out from stage left and drags you away, still screaming invective from the wings.

Poe can help. Dude was a world's authority—he wrote the book on it without even knowing.

Say that, like Poe with Burton, you've grown to hate your boss. Maybe you're feeling "uncontrollable disgust at his [or her] chicanery, arrogance, ignorance and brutality." What you must remember, first of all, is to remain unintimidated. This is an occasion for you to fan your feathers, an all-caps OP-POE-TUNITY. "Believe me," Poe once told a friend, "there exists no such dilemma as that in which a gentleman is placed when he is forced to reply to a blackguard. If he have any genius then is the time for its display."

Consider the following simple conversational moves you can borrow from Poe's letter. Each of them can work in a variety of circumstances, whether you're being confronted in a breakroom, attacked in a group email thread, or better yet, sitting across from the CEO in his or her office, locked in mortal struggle.

Move #1: Imply that the other person is behaving in an undignified manner, that *you* would be horribly embarrassed were you ever to stoop so low. Affect vicarious horror and shame. When in doubt, *gaslight*.

Rhetorical flourishes: "In the first place—your attempts to bully me excite in my mind scarcely any other sentiment than mirth." Possible alternatives: "I can't speak to you when you're like this"; "Do you need a minute?"; "Is this a bad time?"

Poe-tic postures: Bug out your eyes. Allow your jaw to drop. Place your elbow on an arm of the chair as if you're settling in to watch a fireworks display of self-mortification.

Move #2: Appeal to their higher nature while—and this is crucial—implying that they may not have one.

Rhetorical flourishes: "Preserve if you can, the dignity of a gentleman [or a lady]." Also good: "Let's be rational about this for a moment, if we *can*"—meaning, of course, if *they* can.

Poe-tic postures: Rest your chin in your hand. Make your best "active listening" face while allowing a generous hint of sarcasm and exasperated patience to show through.

Move #3: Pretend to be flabbergasted that the person is pissed, *no matter how aware you are of why they're pissed.* Pour as much kerosene in that gas lamp as possible, baby!

Rhetorical flourishes: "As I live, I am utterly unable to say why you are angry, or what true grounds of complaint you have against me."

Poe-tic postures: Shake your head. If sitting, swoon back in your chair. If standing, reel backward, aghast. Clutch your pearls, or, if you have no pearls, wordlessly place your palm flat over your heart in the universal sign for "Who, *me???*"

Move #4: Insinuate that people they trust have expressed unflattering opinions about them.

Rhetorical flourishes: "You are a man [or woman] of impulses; have made yourself, in consequence, some enemies." Also good: starting but not finishing either of the following sentences. "I am in a position of knowing . . ."; "Given the rumors that have been going around. . . ." Crucially, do *not* refer to anything concrete that's actually been said. Just imply that whatever it is, it's extremely damaging. If they try to pin you down, resort to, "I can't bring myself to say the words, but I have a feeling you *know* what I'm talking about."

Poe-tic postures: Assume an expression of intense pity, like, *Oh you poor dear*, or if you're from the South, *Bless your heart*. Make eye contact for no more than a few seconds, then look down at the floor while subtly shaking your head.

Special bonus move: Practice abrupt shifts in tone. This will buy you time as your opponent scrambles to understand your apparent about-face. It will also allow you to play with misdirection and to insert false signals. Never allow the other person to feel they are on a firm footing, like they know with any certainty what is coming next.

Rhetorical flourishes: Utilize a 1:1 ratio of insults to flattery. Playing both good cop and bad cop, veer between praise and condemnation and back again.

Poe-tic postures: Keep changing up your body language from open to closed, warm to cold, like a traffic light on the fritz.

How you deploy these is up to you: you can work through each move in order, or mix them up like a fat Halloween sack of hostilities. Either way, if you've done it all right, at the very least you'll have satisfied your own ego. For now, anyway!

Poe tip #9: Never waste a good feud.
All workplace disputes are OP-POE-TUNITIES
to display your true genius.

In any case, your exit from the workplace is now assured, and you're likely feeling more disillusioned than ever with the horrible business of getting and keeping jobs. The more you learn about such organizations, the more you realize they are set up badly on purpose. That ruining human potential is their fundamental *nature*.

Naturally, you may find yourself entertaining an idea that feels both brand-spanking new and like you've had it in the back of your mind forever: opening your own shop, hoisting your very own red flag. Lucky for you, our beloved antagonist has insights into this process, too. In the next lesson, we'll look at Poe's clever shortcut to CEO status.

How Long Did Poe Work There? A Timeline

If you're ever inclined to feel bad about how you can't hold down steady work—to somehow think it's your fault that you keep getting the boot or bolting for the door—take a look at the length of time Poe spent at all his various gigs, and take heart. Chances are, you've lasted longer at your shit jobs than he did at his.

- *Southern Literary Messenger*, mid-1835 to early 1837 (less than two years)

- *Burton's Gentleman's Magazine*, mid-1839 to mid-1840 (about one year)

- *Graham's Magazine*, early 1841 to early 1842 (just over one year)

- *New York Mirror*, late 1844 to mid-1845 (a few months)

- *The Broadway Journal*, mid-1845 to early 1846 (less than one year)

LESSON #10
Sneaking into the C-Suite

What if you could become a self-made success story, perhaps even the CEO of your own company, while hardly lifting one ink-stained finger? Our mutual friend has a final career lesson for you, and ultimate life hacks simply do not come hackier.

As you may recall, Poe started out wanting to bypass the whole working-stiff thing and instead be a genius poet. So of course he spent the *rest* of his career dreaming of opening his own shop. Just days after he got the axe from *Burton's Gentleman's Magazine* in 1840, he published a prospectus for a magazine of his own—a move he'd been pondering at least since his *Messenger* days. He hated being poor, and knew he'd never realize capitalism's biggest rewards if he kept working for others.

"I have not only labored solely for the benefit of others (receiving for myself a miserable pittance)," as Poe put it, "but have been forced to model my thoughts at the will of men whose imbecility was evident to all but themselves."

That his editor jobs were creative—to a degree anyway—made matters worse, not better. Then as now, knowledge work takes it out of you: "To coin one's brain into silver, at the nod of a master, is to my thinking the hardest task in the world," Poe grumbled, rightly. Add to this the age-old workplace truths—schmucks for bosses, shitty wages—and his desire for the ultimate escape could only grow.

Establishing a magazine of his own became nothing less than "the grand purpose of my life," and as such, it would be no mere kitchen-table undertaking. He wanted to launch the be-all and end-all of American magazines—intellectually sophisticated, beautifully laid out, expensively printed, and free of the "buffoonery, scurrility, or profanity" that characterized all those *other* rags. It would be an extension of his own best self, stamped through with his unerring taste, his unique genius. Also, this magazine was going to bring him a pile of filthy lucre. Yet publishing the prospectus was just the first step in the process. What he needed most was to find "a partner possessing ample capital, and at the same time, so little self-esteem, as to allow me entire control of the editorial conduct."

Poe thought he might've found this individual in George Graham, who in 1841 purchased *Burton's Gentleman's Magazine* and renamed it *Graham's Magazine*, bringing Poe back on as editor yet paying him a good deal more. At $800 a year (a shade under $24,000 today), it would be the highest salary Poe ever earned, so perhaps he was right to hope. Graham, like John Pendleton Kennedy before him, was a kindhearted man who appreciated both Poe's talents and his desperate financial need.

At the same time, as a magazine proprietor himself, Graham could not be expected to act against his own interests and set up a competitor. Surprisingly, finding a deep-pocketed, self-loathing business partner, it turns out, isn't any easier than locating an overgenerous, hands-off patron. Who knew? But Poe never gave up hope. His search for a wealthy backer—for the moolah to get his venture off the ground—would continue throughout the 1840s, until the last days of his life in fact. That final journey he made in 1849, the one that ended with him dying in a Baltimore hospital, was all about drumming up interest in his magazine.

That could seem like the saddest end, like the opposite of victory. And it's true that some of the evidence suggests Poe wouldn't have been so great at running his own magazine. The one time that he got close, the venture folded almost as soon as it began. In 1845, with a combination of borrowed funds and bar-napkin IOUs, he came into ownership of a New York newspaper called *The Broadway Journal*, and he could hardly believe his luck. "By a series of manoeuvres [sic] almost incomprehensible to myself, I have succeeded in getting rid, one by one, of all my associates in "The Broadway Journal", and (as you will see by last week's paper) have now become sole editor and owner," he told his old mentor Kennedy in a letter that October. Somewhat less promisingly, he went on to explain, "I have exhausted all my immediate resources in the purchase—and I now write to ask you for a small loan—say $50." By December, Poe had been forced to sell a partial interest; by January, the *Broadway Journal* was dead, over, finito, kaput.

Running your own business is hard. We glorify those who do it—the Zuckerbergs, the Musks, the Bransons—not always remembering that we're looking at a handful of green shoots in an overall landscape of failure as desolate and gloomy as any Poe described in his fiction. Most start-ups never leave the garage. Most *Shark Tank* contestants disappear, never to be heard from again, as if eaten by actual sharks. Most of us don't have the ruthlessness, the un-medicated mania, and most importantly, the continual access to capital that is required. Scholars generally agree that the reason Poe couldn't hang on to the *Journal* was textbook: he would have had to lose money for a long time before he could make money, and he just didn't have the cash to do that. Few do.

None of this means Poe failed, much less that it's useless or naive to think about starting your own business. It indicates the opposite. The *fantasy* of hanging out your own shingle can sustain you through all the horrendous frustration and struggle of a working life, providing you a crucial outlet for your agita and your grandiosity. And just like Poe, it can lead you to make the ultimate work-life hack: refashioning your self-image in a bold, new direction, *portraying yourself as not just another working slob but as a visionary*. The best part? You don't even have to launch the business to reinvent yourself as said genius! That part's a formality, one you're free to skip.

Here again, Poe's example can guide you. In attempting to establish his magazine in the last decade of his life, he finally wised up and applied his gift of fiction writing to his own résumé. He rewrote his professional history the better to attract potential investors—and it became one of the most powerful, lasting stories he *ever* told.

"I joined the 'Messenger' as you know which was then in its 2d year with 700 subscribers & the general outcry was that because a Magazine had never succeeded South of the Potomac therefore a Magazine never cd [could] succeed," Poe boasted in one would-be fundraising letter. "Yet in despite of this & in despite of the wretched taste of its proprietor which hampered & controlled me at all points I . . . increased the circulation in 15 months to 5,500 subscribers paying an annual profit of 10,000 when I left it."

These and other claims he made about his editorial prowess and contributions to various workplaces would be accepted as true for *the next 150 years*. Talk about a success story, and a literally self-made man! Not until 1999 would the truth come out, with Terence Whalen proving how Poe's contributions were not quite so spectacular. For instance, though Poe implied he grew *Messenger* subscriptions by around 700 percent, the real growth he helped to deliver was a respectable but less eye-popping 40 percent. Poe fudged the numbers skyward because, as Whalen put it, he was engaged in "the deadly serious business of self-fashioning" which induced him to "invent new 'facts' about his past."*

* These are also called "lies."

The obvious question becomes: What new facts can you invent about your past? How can you, too, create a false impression of business genius that lasts the next 150 years? No matter how you may have screwed up your career to date, fear not. You *have* arrived. Only two tiny steps now separate you from the C-suite role of your dreams:

1. Begin by closing your eyes. Lay out in your mind exactly what sort of business you'd establish, how you'd run it, how you'd do everything differently than your current shit boss. Let your imagination run wild—let your ego streak naked and free—with visions of vast personal riches, plus your beneficence and generosity to employees. Imagine that you have the money to do whatever the hell you like, and people around you must indulge you and listen to your bullshit pronouncements no matter what, because their Blue Apron memberships and their kids' $40,000 preschool tuition depends on it. What are they gonna do, tell you you're full of it? Hell no. Their indulgent smiles can't slip an inch. Enjoy.

2. Break out your résumé and juice it up with the patented Poe-tic techniques outlined below on our checklist. Keep in mind that Poe not only lied about vastly increasing subscriptions to the magazines he worked for, he also massaged his job titles, presenting himself in more elevated roles than he in fact occupied. Bonus Poe tip: On occasion, he also shaved a few years off his age to appear more of a wunderkind. The same techniques are available to you.

Now, since you live in a Google-able age, you will want to avoid outright lies, such as claiming specific degrees or professional licenses you don't actually have (because such untruths can have tiresome legal implications). Padding and nest-feathering, however, are harder to call out, and what's better, the line between them and actual lying is as blurry as those letters on the bottom row of a vision test. The point is to focus on unverifiable stats, unfalsifiable claims, and "soft" skills.

A checklist:

O Could you invent some statistics out of thin air? Doesn't matter what they refer to exactly. The presence of several "%" signs alone will make you seem sharp, like you know how to do math.

O Could you make a claim about being "part of a team" that accomplished some tremendous goal, whether or not you personally had anything to do with its accomplishment? Even the janitor at Tesla helps develop electric cars—sort of! Why let petty concerns about scrupulous honesty hold you back? If you think business visionaries trouble themselves with such details, you'll be Swiffering those floors forever.

O Could you be vaguer about dates so as to seem younger, or, on the other end of the spectrum, vastly more experienced than you are? Remember, the capitalist ideal is a twenty-something with decades of experience, so act accordingly.

○ Do you know a pliable former teacher, mentor, or well-placed friend who might be induced to sign off on a glowing testimonial? If so, ask them to write a glowing testimonial. They should not fail to include the words "genius," "wunderkind," and "visionary." Bonus points if this individual just happens to be Bill Gates or Warren Buffett. Or Henry Kissinger, because hey, it worked for Elizabeth Holmes, right? For a while!

○ Absolutely anyone can be a "consultant," a fact you can use to cover up any gaps in your work history—no matter if the only person you were "consulting" was a red-faced, poopy infant, or that gum-snapping receptionist down at the temp agency.

Finally, realize that because you have fantasized at length about having your own business—if only to complete the steps in this lesson—you now have CEO experience. Don't fail to add that to your résumé, too. Poe never managed to get his magazine off the ground, but he did succeed in fooling a lot of people for a long time. Why not you?

Poe tip #10: The point is not to run your own
business, but to portray yourself as a business genius.
Stop at nothing.

Now that you've absorbed all his most salient Poe-fessional lessons, it's
time to move on to that *other* great boondoggle: Sex. Turn the page to
begin Part 3 of the Poe-gram.

PART 3
Sex and Death

Quick priority check: Do you care more about money and career advancement or about love and sex? If you're looking for the richest payload of disappointment, there's only one answer. Thwarted ambitions make you drink, but loss in love makes you want to guzzle oblivion itself, so this is where Poe's role as guru *really* comes into its own. He's now prepared to show you:

- → The art of losing your first love (and your second one, too)
- → Why he never had kids, and the surprising reason you shouldn't, either
- → The pros and cons of sliding into your fans' DMs

Plus, become acquainted with the benefits of galaxy brain, and learn to get the most mileage out of your inevitable nervous breakdown.

How to Lose at Love like a Real Romantic

Rewind the clock a moment. One day, when Poe was about fourteen, his friend Robert Stanard invited him over to his house after school, where Poe met Robert's mother, Jane Stith Stanard, a pale-faced ministering angel, "the first purely ideal love of my soul." It only makes sense. Poe had lost his own mother so early on that his orphan's heart may well have longed for a mother's gentle expression, sympathetic ear, and—what else?—air of inexorable tragedy.

Jane was about thirty. He was still a boy. Nothing romantic could happen, but he could still bathe in her presence, maybe touch her hand. At least, he could until the spring of 1824, when she died, insane.* Poe was fifteen years old.

In later life, Poe would tell the story so many ways that it's impossible to know how many times he met Mrs. Stanard. He told one girlfriend that they met just once. Poe's aunt-and-then-mother-in-law, Maria Clemm, heard a different version. "When Eddie was unhappy at home (which was often the case), he went to her for sympathy," Mrs. Clemm said, "and she always consoled and comforted him." After Jane Stanard's

---

* Honestly, we don't know much more about Jane Stanard's death than this. Did people just die insane all the time in the 1820s? Well, clearly, to an extent.

death, Clemm maintained, Poe and Robert would visit her grave, mourning together through the long, drawn-out evenings.

Poe's second brush with love involved someone more appropriate—in fact, a neighbor close to his own age. Sarah Elmira Royster lived across the street from the Allans for a time. Years later, she is said to have told a Richmond acquaintance: "He was a beautiful boy—Not very talkative. When he did talk though he was pleasant but his general manner was sad." Poe visited her at her house, and sometime before he left for college, the two reached an understanding. He wrote her often from Charlottesville, but she never wrote back. *Not because she was ignoring him.* Because she didn't know he was writing her at all. Elmira's father was intercepting the letters—who can blame him?—maybe because he

thought they were too young to get seriously involved, or more likely because Poe was an adopted son, not an official heir. Elmira, assuming Poe no longer cared for her, turned seventeen and married some rich guy with society connections (and who could blame her?).

Then, guess what? Poe showed up at the wedding like an importunate, freshly dumped ghost—or so he implied in a poem—and saw a "burning blush" come over Elmira's face when she caught sight of him.* It's unlikely Poe was telling the truth, but, as is often the case with him, his "rendition" of the story proves just as revealing. As we know, he was never the type to overlook a personal mythmaking opportunity, or leave undeveloped some supposed encounter with gut-wrenching tragedy. This seems to reflect a *philosophie de l'amour* he was developing, as self-consciously as possible, of course. In another of the poems he claims to have begun writing as a teenager, he said:

> And so, being young and dipt in folly
> I fell in love with melancholy . . .
>
> I could not love except where Death
> Was mingling his with Beauty's breath —
> Or Hymen, Time, and Destiny
> Were stalking between her and me.

To hear him tell it, Poe could only fall in love when a tragic end was a foregone conclusion, or when struggling to overcome such Matterhorn-high hurdles as time, destiny, and meddling parents. Someone dies insane,

---

* God knows what burning sensation might've come over her dad's face.

somebody gets jilted, or GTFO. Love affairs that go nowhere are just . . . basic. The truly evolved person scopes out only those relationships that must necessarily end in grief. Otherwise, where's the spark? Also, this way you don't have to splash out so much on Valentine's Day tchotchkes and tequila sodas.

Whether Poe was being sincere or melodramatic, this line of thinking was characteristic of his era. You could say the big artistic and intellectual mood of the first half of the nineteenth century was all about experience and imagination. Feelings triumphed over reason, dogma, tradition, religion—basically, over whatever your stodgy dad believed. Both Poe and his own youthful antihero, George Gordon, Lord Byron (the wildly promiscuous, bisexual, own-half-sister-banging poet), lived out their Romantic values, and then some.

When they weren't swooning, they were grieving. When they weren't grieving, they were swooning (to get over the grief). They understood themselves to contain both man's greatness *and* his wretchedness, and they were obsessed with obsession, love, youth, nature, fate, loss, despair, death, and such weird, floating states as might lie beyond death. But what else could they do, given the combination of rampant infectious disease and lack of medical understanding in those days, the absurdly shitty romantic, sexual, and existential odds they had no choice but to brave out?

Their kind of Romantic heroism, as historian Jacques Barzun argued, wasn't just a melodramatic display. Instead it was a courageous, life-affirming response to the awful problems of their age, arguably of *every* age—no matter how tawdry and sordid it may have appeared at times. "The fact that romantic lives also show a seamy side or a want of calmness is therefore no diminuation of the heroism," Barzun said, "on the contrary it is the drabness and the anguish that make life heroic."

What's this got to do with you? Everything. Thankfully, people don't die young in the same numbers nowadays, yet *your* likely trajectory of years of wistfully swiping right, possibly leading up to a historically late marriage or no marriage at all, means you're no more insulated from crushed hopes or romantic failures or lost loves than Poe or Byron ever was. Here, masticate on some facts.

- While the research is spotty, limited surveys suggest the average age of first love is between fifteen and eighteen.

- According to CDC data, as of 2015, the average man aged twenty-five to forty-four has had 6.1 sexual partners (of the opposite sex, anyway). A woman of the same age has had 4.2.*

- The same data show that 21 percent of men aged fifteen to forty-four, and 10 percent of women of the same age, have had more than fifteen partners.

- The average age of first marriage in the United States is twenty-seven for a woman and twenty-nine for a man.

- The American Psychological Association reports that 40 to 50 percent of first marriages end in divorce, with the divorce rate significantly higher in subsequent marriages.

Eyeball the landscape, and you'll see: pain is inevitable. Why not take the Romantics' view, Poe's view, and prepare to glory in your despair?

---

* Take it from me: you can forget the other four. The best sex is always with that two-tenths of a person.

Stockpile the tissues—and the Stoli, and the Cherry Garcia. Line up the rebounds.

Your first love is the natural place to start. When it comes to this pivotal initial relationship, the best strategy is to lead with bitter experience—to lose your first love in the most spectacular possible fashion. The worse the loss, the less likely you are to ever get over it, and at one go you will have calibrated your romantic expectations for the rest of your life *right down to zero where they belong.* Voilà!

Staying with your first love may in fact be the riskier proposition. Is it even possible to be happy forever in that way you envisioned in your "purely ideal" teenage years? Nope. If you stayed together, you'd soon be doing laundry together, raising children together, paying quarterly estimated taxes together. Grim practicalities would soon set in, over a period of years slowly strangling your original hopes. You'd get tired of the person—you'd find out they weren't so wonderful and perfect after all.

But if you lose them early on, then you'll become convinced they were special and irreplaceable, and you'll long to be with them, and you won't be able to be with them, and not only will you have given yourself ample material for terrible, angsty poetry, you'll have tapped into a grand cultural tradition, a rite of passage every bit as important as a first kiss or losing your virginity. What is this magical rite? Looking them up online years later, and marveling at how he's already lost his hair or how much weight she's gained, then *breathing a sigh of relief at the bullet you dodged.*

You don't have to experience early romantic losses on Poe's scale, either, to get the salutary effect. Your first love need not have died

95

insane in 1824, or have married someone else at seventeen, though it helps. Do not worry. You can be disappointed by much less shocking developments. Any adolescence can provide the right raw ingredients, because youths and young adults need only scant encouragement to experience new phenomena in a powerful way. "All wonder is the effect of novelty upon ignorance," as Dr. Johnson once said. That is, the lack of precedent will create the drama. So long as your experiences leave you feeling doomed, depressed, bereft, haunted, and hopeless, then you're on your way.

Even if you don't write poetry and don't want to, you'll still have material enough for every secret smile that you ever smile at weddings, or at young couples making out on the subway, or when gazing over at some married couple eating dinner together in hostile silence. You will *know*. You may never grow wiser about love. Poe didn't, as the rest of his love life, as seen in the following lessons, demonstrates. But, crucially, it is possible at least to feel resigned to your fate.

In an 1839 letter, Poe told a friend, "It makes me laugh to hear you speaking about 'romantic young persons' as of a race with whom, for the future, you have nothing to do. You need not attempt to shake off or to banter off Romance. It is an evil you will never get rid of to the end of your days. It is a part of yourself—a portion of your soul. Age will only mellow it a little, and give it a holier tone."

This is what you must tell yourself every time you feel your hopes stirring. Amorous longing is an evil you'll never get rid of. It's a part of yourself, a portion of your soul. Age will mellow it only a little and give it a holier tone.* Or, in modern terms:

Poe tip #11: No crush is too pathetic, no romantic prospect too weird, inappropriate, or obviously doomed, to get your hopes up just one more time. Lean on in, and don't expect it to end well.

For more on inappropriate love objects and worse behavior, turn the page. Many fans know Edgar Allan Poe married his first cousin, Virginia Clemm, when she was not yet fourteen years old. What most people don't know is that, in wooing his bride, Poe wheedled, cajoled, stretched the truth, and threatened suicide.

As "meet cute" stories go, this one's killer.

---

* This is the *only* part of you that will become more toned as you age.

A Love Poem Fill-in-the-Blank

Need help wooing some doomed prospect, say, your current office crush or an attractive neighbor? Use Poe's "To Helen" as a template to write your own great love poem. Well, a poem anyway.

_____ , thy _____ is to me
　THEIR NAME　　　　NOUN

Like those_____ _____ of yore,
　　　　　ADJECTIVE　PLURAL NOUN

That gently, o'er a perfumed _____,
　　　　　　　　　　　　　NOUN

The _____ , _____
　　ADJECTIVE　　ADJECTIVE

To _____ own native _____.
　PRONOUN　　　　　　NOUN

On desperate _____ long wont to _____
　　　　　PLURAL NOUN　　　　　　　VERB

Thy _____ hair, thy _____ face,
　ADJECTIVE　　　　　ADJECTIVE

Thy _____ airs have brought me home
　ADJECTIVE

To the glory that was _____,
　　　　　　　　　NAME OF A COUNTRY

And the grandeur that was _____.
　　　　　　　　　　NAME OF A CITY

Lo! in yon brilliant _____
　　　　　　HOUSEHOLD OBJECT (e.g., FIREPLACE)

How _____-like I see thee stand,
　NOUN

The _____ within thy hand!
　NOUN

Ah, _____, from the regions which
　NAME OF A GOD OR GODDESS

Are _____!
　NAME OF SACRED PLACE

Pathological Mate Selection

It was many and many a year ago—August of 1835, Richmond. Poe, aged twenty-six, had moved back down from Baltimore to start his first big job at the *Messenger*, solving his money/career problem and stumbling into a different, more insidious dilemma: loneliness. He missed the poor yet affectionate household he'd left behind, including his paternal aunt Maria and his young cousin Virginia. When he got wind that another cousin, Neilson Poe, had offered to take one or both of these ladies to live in his own household, Poe flipped out. Convinced he would never see Virginia again, he sent off an aching, terrified, pleading, repetitive, and possibly drunken letter, addressed to his aunt, but intended for Virginia to read, too. She had just turned thirteen.

"My last my last my only hold on life is cruelly torn away—I have no desire to live and *will not*," Poe swore. "But let my duty be done. I love, *you know* I love Virginia passionately devotedly. I cannot express in words the fervent devotion I feel towards my dear little cousin—my own darling." The torrent ran on and on. "You have both tender hearts—and you will always have the reflection that my agony is more than I can bear—that you have driven me to the grave—for love like mine can never be gotten over."

Carrying on alone was beyond him. "What have I *to live for*?" he asked. "Among strangers with *not one soul to love me*." What a shame, too, that the sweet little house with a garden that he had found for the three of them on Richmond's Church Hill must go unoccupied, and this when he'd secured it for such an advantageous rent.* Poe was earning more than enough at the *Messenger* to support the household, he claimed, and as his wife, Virginia would have the chance to enter into society. Now, alas, the dream was over. Unless Maria and Virginia would reconsider?

In a postscript, Poe spelled out the warning one last time: "My love, my own sweetest Sissy, my darling little wifey, think well before you break the heart of your Cousin, Eddy."

Reading this in the twenty-first century, you cringe. It's like a thirty car pile-up of taboos. Where even to begin?

- ➤ We don't smile at adults wooing thirteen-year-olds.

- ➤ The idea of first-cousin marriages is icky now (though not as illegal as you'd think).

- ➤ Threats of suicide rightly strike us as more manipulative than romantic.

- ➤ "Sissy."

- ➤ Also, for the love of God, "wifey." Ugh.

Still, let's size up Poe's motives for a moment. At this point in his life, he had almost no living family. By 1835, Poe had lost his biological parents, his foster parents, his older brother, Henry, and he now believed he stood to lose his aunt and cousin. Virginia was *very* young, even by the standards of the day, yet there's no suggestion, either before or after his marriage, that Poe pursued young girls as a matter of course. In fact,

---

* It's unclear whether the sweet little house existed, or if Poe made it up. I have my suspicions. How 'bout you?

he rarely if ever operated like a guy on the prowl.* The infantile shrieking of his letter strongly suggests he was acting more out of raw, blind emotional need. And *that* is something we all do when selecting our own mates, much as we may want to deny it. And what's more, it can work. It *did* work. His aunt approved the match, and he and Virginia married. Sooner or later.

More on those nuptials in a moment. You might still wonder how such a desperate and misguided suitor could teach us anything about love and long-term partnership. It's because his methods touch on

---

* W. H. Auden's crack that Poe's love life was "largely confined to crying in laps," like all good putdowns, lands close to the truth.

certain essential truths, one of which was explained by Charles Darwin. We all know about Darwin's law of natural selection. A second, less well known Darwinian law is sexual selection, or the sexual competition that takes places within a single species, and not just yellow-rumped warblers and alkali bees.

Like other animals, humans select mates in part on the basis of reproductive fitness. Our psychology has evolved so that we often (though hardly always) *prefer* partners who help us maximize our own reproductive potential. This explains why some of us are compelled by, say, certain waist-to-hip ratios and/or single men in possession of a good fortune. Where conditions allow, many people also prefer partners with whom they can develop what evolutionary psychologists term "an intimate and emotionally satisfying relationship." And it is here where things can turn wack.

Why? Because what plucks our heartstrings, what smacks to us of deep intimacy, may be weird, dark, even downright disturbing. This is because we often seek, consciously or unconsciously, to recreate the emotional conditions in which we grew up, and such tastes come from a place beyond logic's reach. "We may choose friendships based on common interests and complementary qualities, but our reasons for falling in love are altogether more irrational, projections of our most infantile wants and pathology," as the writer Tim Kreider put it. "Our lovers are summoned up by the most primal and naked part of ourselves. Introducing these people to our friends and family is, in a way, more heedlessly exhibitionistic than posting nude photos or sex tapes of ourselves online; it's like letting everyone watch our uncensored dreams."

Be honest. How many of your friends' or siblings' or colleagues' couplings *don't* make you wonder—and shiver—in private? Chances are, they're having the same reaction to *your* relationship. Look at anyone hustling to the altar and try to say they're in a state of *mental clarity.* You'll laugh. And laugh. And laugh. Of all our fantasies about love, partnership, and marriage, the sheer biggest must be the one that says we choose our mates because we both like to rock-climb and have great sex. Some kind of shared past or shared pathology is more like it.

But let's agree that your choice of love objects is going to be strange in some less troubling way than Poe's—that your preferences are eyebrow-raising, rather than statute-breaking. You still face the same problem we all face: there isn't one right person for you. Instead, there are numerous wrong people you could or will end up with, though some will be less wrong than others. And you don't have a lifetime to spend sorting them out. Since the average age of marriage in the United States today is twenty-seven for a woman and twenty-nine for a man, even if you begin your search for a mate at fifteen, then women have just a dozen years to sort through billions of potential partners, while men have fourteen years to do the same.* Yet those two extra years can make no practical difference. The task is impossible on its face. It is where sheer unlikelihood runs headlong into your skill at self-deceit, recalling *The Onion* headline: "18-Year-Old Miraculously Finds Soul-Mate in Hometown."

Tweak this header and you get "Lonely and Impoverished 27-Year-Old Finds Soul-Mate in 13-Year-Old Cousin." A month after he sent that crazed letter, Poe returned to Baltimore and took out a marriage

---

* That is, at least until you hit the statistical average.

license for himself and Virginia. The following May, in 1836, they were wed in what some biographers believe was merely the official ceremony (with some arguing that there may have been an earlier, secret wedding). Virginia wasn't quite fourteen. Her age was changed to twenty-one on the marriage certificate, perhaps because two witnesses were needed and only one came. Perhaps for, uh, other reasons.

In all, it's the kind of biographical humdinger that makes this writer want to recede into a hedge. Yet there's plenty of evidence that the Poes loved each other with a love that, if not more than love, was profound and devoted on both sides. Poe splashed out his meager funds on music lessons for Virginia and loved to hear her sing. "Ever with thee I wish to roam," she told him in a poem she wrote one Valentine's Day, "Dearest, my life is thine." And it is impossible to read the sole surviving letter that Poe wrote her without blinking back tears of your own. "In my last great disappointment, I should have lost my courage *but for you*—my little darling wife," he told her in 1846. "You are my *greatest* and *only* stimulus now. . . ."

They managed somehow, and maybe that should not surprise us. We all marry the wrong person, argues the contemporary philosopher Alain de Botton: "Marriage ends up as a hopeful, generous, infinitely kind gamble taken by two people who don't know yet who they are or who the other might be, binding themselves to a future they cannot conceive of and have carefully avoided investigating."

That sounds like a bar to something working out, but it isn't. A long-term romantic relationship is fundamentally a living arrangement, an organizing principle about affection and groceries and real estate and what to watch on Netflix as you fall asleep. It follows that a good marriage is like finding the best possible roommate, someone who is not so irresponsible that one day the city "just happens" to cut off your electricity from unpaid bills, and whom you want to have lots of sex with. Any such arrangement is going to be inflected with your own particular pathology and your partner's, which means that sometimes it'll feel so warm and familiar as to seem, dare I say it, natural—a Hallmark card for as many as two or three afternoons per year. Sometimes, too, it'll also be the cause of you gritting your teeth, feeling your blood pressure spike in a groove so well worn it might've come preinstalled. "Goddamn it," you mutter, hunting for your flashlight in the dark. "This again."

Don't let other people's personal PR campaigns fool you. The fact that everyone on Facebook is apparently married to their best friend and "partner in crime"—crime meaning taco nights, a Chevy Tahoe, megachurch attendance, and one-point-seven children holding up those fancy chalkboards that say things like FIRST DAY OF FIFTH GRADE!!—alone suggests a convenient social lie, like nearly all other social-media claims.

On Twitter, realtors, financiers, and military generals all chirp in their bios that they are "happily married," while some CEOs and former US presidents lead their personal blurbs with "husband, father," carefully mentioning these before their well-known public roles, as if to tell you where their priorities really lie. Who are they trying to convince, and why, and can't they hear themselves? You can try to gloss over the weirdness of your romantic and sexual tastes, but Poe offers the better strategy: marry someone inappropriate enough and the resulting scandal may last 170 years and counting, stoking endless fascination with your life. Win-win!

Poe tip #12: Don't bother seeking a soulmate. Let your insecurities and pathologies lead the way.

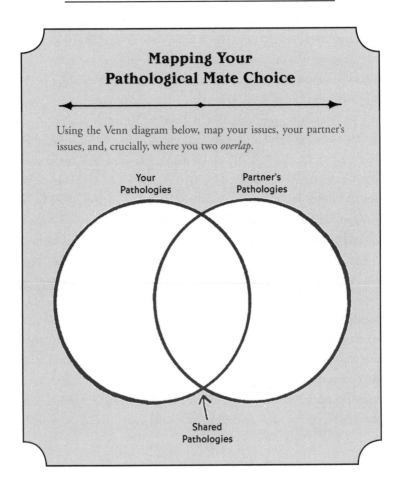

Mapping Your Pathological Mate Choice

Using the Venn diagram below, map your issues, your partner's issues, and, crucially, where you two *overlap*.

Your
Pathologies

Partner's
Pathologies

Shared
Pathologies

Poe-creation

Here's something you might not know about Poe's century: between 1800 and 1900, the birthrate among white married couples in America fell by almost 50 percent. Couples went from having an average of seven children to fewer than four. The rate of extramarital pregnancy also plummeted, dropping from a late 1700s peak of 30 percent to around 10 percent by the mid-1800s, about the time Poe died. Demographic changes don't come much bigger, so though you might not associate Poe's era with sexual revolution, you could. As the theorist Michel Foucault and the historian Estelle Freedman have both argued, the nineteenth century may *not* have been the repressed, buttoned-up epoch we so often take it to be. The spread of relatively effective birth control techniques meant that sex could serve different purposes.* You could have sex to make babies. Or, you could have sex to express yourself. You could have sex for fun.

Poe and Virginia were married for over a decade, but never had any babies of their own. Some critics have used this fact as a jumping-off point to theorize that Poe must have been impotent, or otherwise sexually dysfunctional, quite possibly into "sado-necrophilia."† If anything, the evidence runs the other way. Poe's 1842 short story *"Eleonora"* is about a

---

* Bear in mind that plenty else happened in the century that might've affected the birth rate, including urbanization, war, and that trend in mutton-chop sideburns which (presumably) turned off many women.

† Or all three, who knows?

pair of cousins who grow up together in a cozy valley, with one passage in particular often read as a keyhole view into the Poes' bedchamber. And while, reader, I share your dread of long quotes, you *have* to read the passage to get the entire erotic effect. Behold the closest thing Poe ever wrote to a porno:

> Hand in hand about this valley, for fifteen years, roamed I with Eleonora before Love entered within our hearts. It was one evening . . . that we sat, locked in each other's embrace, beneath the serpent-like trees, and looked down within the waters of the River of Silence at our images therein. We spoke no words during the rest of that sweet day; and our words even upon the morrow were tremulous and few. We had drawn the God Eros from that wave, and now we felt that he had enkindled within us the fiery souls of our forefathers. The passions which had for centuries distinguished our race, came thronging with the fancies for which they had been equally noted, and together breathed a delirious bliss over the Valley of the Many-Colored Grass.

After the cousins discover "Eros," everything is different. The world rings with life like a Wagner opera—say, *Tristan und Isolde*.

> A change fell upon all things. Strange brilliant flowers, star-shaped, burst out upon the trees where no flowers had been known before. The tints of the green carpet deepened; and when, one by one, the white daisies shrank away, there sprang up, in place of them, ten by ten of the ruby-red asphodel. And

life arose in our paths; for the tall flamingo, hitherto unseen, with all gay glowing birds, flaunted his scarlet plumage before us. The golden and silver fish haunted the river, out of the bosom of which issued, little by little, a murmur that swelled, at length, into a lulling melody more divine than that of the harp of Aeolus—sweeter than all save the voice of Eleonora. And now, too, a voluminous cloud, which we had long watched in the regions of Hesper, floated out thence, all gorgeous in crimson and gold, and settling in peace above us, sank, day by day, lower and lower, until its edges rested upon the tops of the mountains, turning all their dimness into magnificence, and shutting us up, as if forever, within a magic prison-house of grandeur and of glory.

You wouldn't call this stuff explicit or confessional, and yet locked embraces, thronging fancies, delirious bliss, swelling murmurs, even—maybe especially—how Poe makes that analogy of erotic life to "a magic prison-house of grandeur and of glory"? Make no mistake. We're talking about boning.

Poe appears to imply, in lush yet polite terms, that he and Virginia did know at least a throb or three of sexual joy. He implies, furthermore, that this joy might not have begun on their wedding night—it may have been more of a later development, possibly a few years in. But if the Poes did have an active sex life, why didn't they have children, and what can their lives teach you about how to make (or avoid making) one of the most momentous commitments there is?

There was no Ortho Tri-Cyclen in their day, no Nuvaring or Tutti-Frutti-flavored Trojans. The precise cellular mechanism by which babies are made was unknown to science, though certain devices and techniques were understood to be preventative, from crude and expensive condoms made from animal skins, to douching, to abortifacient pills (that is, pills advertised in a coded way as likely to induce miscarriage), to actual abortions (broadly legal until the 1880s).* Not all these methods are reliable, nor can we assume every couple had them ready at hand in their nightstand drawers.

Still, Poe was a man of the world. He had a seafaring, globe-trotting older brother, he'd served in the military himself, and his reading life included not just the newspapers and magazines of his day but a great

---

* Granted, you could also get rubber condoms after about 1840. Call it a blowout century for condom technology.

deal of medicine, science, and history. Assuming he and Virginia were fertile for at least a portion of their marriage, maybe their choice to not become parents was deliberate. To be clear: this is just a hunch I have, a matter of speculation, but one worth drawing out just the same.

You don't need a biologist to tell you that—misty-eyed grandparents' fantasies notwithstanding—reproduction is *not designed* to make you happy. Its function is to perpetuate the species. So, as with mate selection, this may not be an arena in which we make decisions based altogether on straightforward, fully conscious, rational considerations—which has a way of making the issue all the more complex and difficult. Modern life offers reliable ways to choose the moment we reproduce (or not), and a much greater element of choice even than in Poe's time. If you're confused and anxious about whether to have kids or not, no wonder. We're not really equipped to *think* our way out of this one. That's why it can be helpful to imagine why the Poes may have abstained. Let's consider three possible reasons:

1. Money

How poor are you now? Would you like to be even poorer? If you've read the section of this book on career and Poe-sonal finance, then you know that the Poes scraped by on his patchy freelance income and grueling, low-wage editorial jobs—so low-wage that they were sometimes scarcely able to eat. You have to think any further strain on their finances might've sunk them altogether. Consider, too, that as expensive as child-raising might've been in the mid-1800s, there's no doubt it's more expensive now. Not only have pesky child labor laws emerged to prevent you from hiring out your kids at the mill, bringing in some extra cash, but Poe and Virginia were never going to have to fork out for Tae Kwon Do lessons, STEM camp, and/or SAT-prep classes. Even if you believe such bougie concerns are nice-to-haves, not need-to-haves, diapers alone may break the bank. A newborn will soil up to a dozen pricey Pampers a day. And your economic obligation doesn't end at the potty-training stage. If the trend of prolonged adolescence and late-blooming continues, you may be looking at a financial commitment equivalent to a thirty-year mortgage beyond any other debt you may be carrying. Plus an unshaven twenty-something perpetually occupying that guestroom you'd *really* prefer to use as a home gym.

2. Excess capacity and conditions of overload

Whatever you choose to do with your life will expand to take up almost all your time. Though he never made millions at it, Poe was hugely devoted to his career, always hustling on his ambitious artistic and commercial dreams (and his professional rivalries). Amid his efforts, though, Virginia's health began to fail. She first showed the signs of tuberculosis in January of 1842, or about six years after the wedding. Tuberculosis can affect fertility, and then there are the possible secondary effects of grave illness to consider: The Poes may have believed Virginia's health too delicate to risk pregnancy, and the touch-and-go nature of her condition may've affected their sex life as well.* In any case, there cannot have been a lot of capacity left over for the raising of children, or for much else at all. How much spare capacity do you have in your own life, and how overloaded do you want to be? Bear in mind that it is not really possible to discover a happy medium between having too little to occupy yourself with and way, way too much. Nature abhors a vacuum, after all, and this is never more true than when it comes to your to-do list.

3. Existential concerns

It's common for people to hope that some part of them will last even after they die, and for most folks, that means their child or children. Yet the Poes seem not to have leaned into this aspect of human nature. Children rarely figure in Poe's work, or when they do, they tend to be the reincarnated spirits of their dead mothers. In Poe's 1835 short story "Morella," the narrator's wife curses her husband even as she expires in childbirth. "When my spirit departs shall the child live—thy child and mine, Morella's. But thy days shall be days of sorrow," she swears, telling her husband happiness: Yeah, that's all over now. By age ten, their baby girl has grown to become the uncanny image of her mother, talking just like her mother, too, and when the narrator finally baptizes her, *she dies.* All in all, you never see Poe regarding kids as the ideal plan for leaving

---

* There's a form of tuberculosis that affects the genitals, is sometimes coincident with pulmonary tuberculosis, and can cause female infertility. What's more, as grim as this is to contemplate, considering how little food they had at times, nutrition may have been a factor as well, affecting one or both Poes.

behind a wholesome, enduring legacy. Instead, he placed his bet on his work surviving him. You may wish to consider whether you want your children or your cultural contributions to survive—it's possible, too, that you may just be mired in some barely subconscious longing for death, which makes you not want to procreate at all. Fair!

Poe tip #13: Don't have kids. They'll probably be the reincarnated spirits of your dead lovers.

Now that Poe has helped us deal with marriage, mortgages, and children, we turn to their sister (cousin?) subject: not the blatant, moaning infidelity of soap operas, but the more common, difficult-to-parse gray zone of mild infractions. You may believe your shady, shameful online flirtations with attractive strangers represent something new. In truth, this is an old story—at least as old as 1845, anyway.

A Poe-creation Checklist

←———————————◆———————————→

As Poe knew, one of the worst problems a new parent can face is their child turning out to be the reincarnated spirit of a long-dead lover. You may have your suspicions, but how can you be sure? Before you move on to the next lesson, answer the following questions. A score of 0 to 3, you're probably safe. A score of 4 or above, look out.

Does your child:

O Grow strangely in stature and intelligence? (1 point)

O Have a smile like their mother's or father's, even to the point of "perfect identity"? (1 point)

O Have eyes that look into the depths of your soul with "intense and bewildering meaning"? (1 point)

O Utter "phrases and expressions of the dead"? (1 point)

O Remain nameless until the age of ten, responding only to "my love" or "my child"? (1 point)

O Experience fiery convulsions of the facial features, their complexion overspread with the "hues of death"? (1 point)

O Ever fall prostrate on the black slabs of your ancestral vault? (2 points)

O Finally, when you go to lay the child in the tomb where your dead love is buried, has the body of your dead lover *disappeared, leaving no trace?* (Very bad sign! 10 points)

Sliding into Their DMs (and Other Disasters)

One day in early 1842, Virginia Poe fell gravely ill. She was singing, then a blood vessel burst in her throat: a dread sign. Everyone knew what the consumption was, and how it must end, though of course no one could say just when that end might come.

For Poe, it was a nightmarish replay of his mother's illness. People with tuberculosis don't just stop breathing and die. Over a long period, breathing becomes more difficult, a more painful struggle. So Virginia lingered, recovering a little and then sickening again, recovering a little and then sickening *again*, over and over for the next five years.

Each time, Poe would despair of her life and mourn her loss, only to get his hopes up once more. Anyone who has ever witnessed a loved one suffer from a terminal illness will recognize the horrible teeter-totter, the gut-wrenching up-and-down emotional lurch, the way you tilt between sorrow and fear and faint hope, and how, sometimes, your nerves stretched to breaking, you almost long for that final release. Both your loved one's and your own. *Take thy beak from out my heart,* you want to whisper.

Poe wrote "The Raven" three years into Virginia's illness, two years before her death. Not coincidentally, it bears the marks of grieving one's great love, knowing they are beyond the reach of hope and, by the same token, knowing one's own self is now beyond the reach of hope, too. Even the afterlife holds no promise.

> "Prophet!" said I, "thing of evil!—prophet still, if bird or devil!
> By that heaven that bends above us—by that God we
>   both adore—
> Tell this soul with sorrow laden if, within the distant Aidenn,
> It shall clasp a sainted maiden whom the angels name Lenore—
> Clasp a rare and radiant maiden whom the angels name Lenore."
> Quoth the Raven "Nevermore."

The public went wild. Periodicals across the country and in Europe ran and reran the poem, and tens of thousands of people thrilled to its dark, hypnotic rhythms, its undertow of relentless sadness and almost glamorous doom. Not for the first time in his career, or the last, Poe had managed to articulate something arresting, true, and universal about the human experience. And he'd packaged it inside a pop hit. His fiction had given him a modest reputation; "The Raven" made him a celebrity.

Poe had known all along that "The Raven" would prove a sensation, and he was pleased and flattered to finally receive the attention he felt he'd long deserved. It was 1845, and the Poe family was living just outside New York City, on what is now the Upper West Side but then was just farmland. Invitations to literary events and parties poured in. Poe found himself the object of respect, sympathy, admiration, and fascination—some of it from women, and not all of it merely friendly. Or discreet.

The poet Frances Sargent Osgood later claimed that Poe asked to be introduced to *her*—because *he* was such a fan of *her* work, she said—though it was probably the other way around. Many years later, she recalled their first meeting: "With his proud and beautiful head erect, his dark eyes flashing with the electric light of feeling and of thought, a peculiar, an inimitable blending of sweetness and hauteur in his expression and manner, he greeted me, calmly, gravely, almost coldly," she gushed, "yet with so marked an earnestness that I could not help being deeply impressed by it."

Thomas Dunn English, another writer acquainted with both Poe and Osgood (and who, it must be said, was in the end no great fan of either), would recall Osgood "doing the infantile act" at one gathering, "seated on a footstool, her face upturned to Poe."

Poe and Osgood began to exchange letters, their correspondence spilling over into the pages of the *Broadway Journal*, and raising eyebrows all over town. Why would they carry on like that in public, you ask? What the freaking eff, you say? To which *I* say, only God knows why, and believe me, I feel you. But for whatever reason, Poe published the gooey poems that Osgood more or less openly addressed to him, and he replied with poems more or less openly addressing her:*

Beloved! amid the earnest woes
That crowd around my earthly path—
(Drear path, alas! where grows
Not even one lonely rose)—
My soul at least a solace hath
In dreams of thee, and therein knows
An Eden of bland repose.

And thus thy memory is to me
Like some enchanted far-off isle
In some tumultuous sea—
Some ocean throbbing far and free
With storms—but where meanwhile
Serenest skies continually
Just o're that one bright island smile.

---

* Okay, so it's not a declaration of love. At the same time, it's not quite neutral. (Nor is it Poe's best work. In fact, he was recycling some old material.)

Virginia Poe, for her part, seems to have encouraged the quasi-romantic mutual regard between Osgood and her husband. She hosted Osgood at their home, and Osgood would later claim that Virginia positively *liked* her influence on Poe, that it kept him from drinking. The fracas seems to have arisen when yet another fan entered the fray. Details are *murky* to say the least, but here's what we think we know.

Elizabeth Ellet was a prolific writer who frequented the same salons and soirees. She also knew both Poe and Osgood—and perhaps did not relish how close the two had become. Visiting Virginia at the Poes' home, Ellet apparently glimpsed an intimate letter that Osgood had written Poe. Expressing grave concern for Osgood's reputation—i.e., shit-stirring—Ellet encouraged Osgood to get her letters back from Poe and thus safeguard her honor. Poe responded that Ellet ought to take a good look at the indiscreet letters she *herself* had been writing to him. So Ellet, aghast, asked her brother—who believed Poe had unfairly impugned his sister's reputation—to retrieve *her own* apparently flirty letters. Poe, thinking he was about to fight a duel with Ellet's brother, went to borrow a pistol from Thomas Dunn English (who may have had his *own* thing for Ellet), but in the process Poe and English somehow got into a fistfight.* Later, Poe would say he'd won the dust-up, that someone had to drag him away from English's "prostrate and rascally carcase" out of fear for English's life. Poe *would* say that, wouldn't he?

Word flew, rumors spread. Everyone got their names dragged through the dirt. The slew of social invitations slowed, and Poe decided it might be

---

* We don't know how or why the fistfight got going, but it's worth asking: How often do these things happen when drinking isn't involved?

a good moment to remove himself and his family from what Virginia once called "the tattling of many tongues." They upped stakes again, moving farther out of the city, eventually renting a small cottage in what is now the Bronx. Ellet faded out of Poe's life, and he and Osgood never met in person again after 1847—probably for the best.

Yet we can relate. Who hasn't impulsively direct-messaged that intriguing person we've glimpsed online, our current domestic arrangement and relationship status notwithstanding? Who isn't vulnerable to the flattery of an attractive stranger's supposedly friendly interest? Who isn't pleased to find their own messages promptly, playfully returned? Who doesn't enjoy a little rom-com-ish volley over the net of Twitter, Facebook, Instagram, Hangouts, text, email, whatever? You tell yourself it's innocent—Poe and Osgood surely told themselves the same thing—and you're thrilled by a response, drawn in by the other person's own obvious, yet coy, enjoyment of the flirtation. Before you know it, you're hooked on checking some inbox, or actual mailbox, depending on the century.

The pros are clear enough:

- You get to show off your charms all over again, to break out all your best lines, best anecdotes. Your current partner has heard all these already—in fact, their smile tightens with a held-back scream every time you tell that one story . . . whereas the new person delights in it. You're free to present only your cutest, cleverest self, your best angles;

- At least you're not *cheating*-cheating. No one's saying you couldn't commit much more serious crimes.

The cons are less clear, especially at the outset, though they have an annoying way of becoming clearer (and harder to ignore) the longer The Thing goes on. Putting them succinctly:

- ➤ The potential for embarrassment when private messages become public;

- ➤ The loss of credibility; how one's current partner is justified in their irritation when they find out, the moral right being, tediously, on their side;

- ➤ How there's both too little at stake (what are you getting out of this?) and too much (what do you stand to lose?), considering the risk you take.

Unfortunately, you're fooling no one. Osgood's friendly overtures weren't merely friendly—she was feeling out for a place in Poe's affections, maybe hoping to feel, uh, something else after that. Likewise, it seems clear that on some level Poe was flattered and hooked on the attention. Were they just indulging a romantic urge, probably committing an only kind-of bad, sort-of sin? Yes. But didn't their indiscretion—*flirting via newspaper*—enlarge the offense? The same goes for you, me, and all the other very online, very self-deceiving saps. That is, everyone.

Bizarrely, full-fledged affairs tend to be handled with more discretion, perhaps because risks are more in line with rewards, such as they may be. Poe's example is, once again, instructive. Try not to do this. Keep it private if you must. Hell, if you're going to be a fool and ruin everything, you might want to realize some actual burning caresses instead.

Poe tip #14: Carry on indiscreetly, and you may have
to flee to the Bronx to staunch the rumors. Beware.

As it turns out, Poe's textual liaisons while married would serve as a mere dry run for the madness—romantic and otherwise—that came after Virginia's death in 1847. He grieved so deeply, and wanted another woman to take care of him so badly, that he embarked on an arguably far more embarrassing string of quasi-affairs, with his grief eventually spilling over into a space opera of metaphysical mania. Let's discuss how you, too, might maximize your nervous breakdown.

Com-Poe-sing Your
Inappropriate DM

Think of everything you want to say to that interesting person you've glimpsed online or IRL. Write it down, type it up. Let it all hang out. Embarrass yourself. Be overeager and gushing and sincere. And then—this is key—*don't send it.*

Galaxy Brain, or Making the Most of Your Nervous Breakdown

If you're going to have a nervous breakdown anyway, make it a spectacular one, complete with gawking audience and baffled fans. This is the lesson of Edgar Allan Poe's sheer strangest major work by far, *Eureka*. He wrote it in the year after Virginia's death, arguably the most grief-stricken time in his grief-stricken life. It's a 40,000-word prose poem about astrophysics. A space opera about love, time, death, and the meaning of existence. A total meltdown writ large and performed for Poe's admiring public.

Virginia Poe's last months on earth were grueling. A family friend visited the Poes at their Bronx cottage in the fall of 1846, describing a scene "dreadful to see." In a tiny, ground-floor bedroom, sometimes too weak to speak, Virginia lay dying. The weather was cold, the room as cold. Struggling to keep her warm, Poe had wrapped Virginia in his old army coat and the family cat lay curled up on her sunken, heaving chest. There was no money for any other comforts to soothe or ease her passage. All Poe could do was stay by her side. "The coat and the cat were the sufferer's only means of warmth," the friend recalled, "except as her husband held her hands, and her mother her feet."

Finally, in January of 1847, Virginia Poe died. She was twenty-four years old—the same age as Poe's mother when she died, the same age as Poe's brother when he died.

Knocked past the limits of his endurance, Poe collapsed. But within the year a strange new spirit—an all-consuming new idea—possessed him. In fact, it was nothing less than his very own grand unifying theory of the physical, metaphysical, mathematical, material, and spiritual universe, and if he left anything out it was not for want of trying. Poe had long been interested in science, keeping abreast of the latest discoveries and theories of his age, and now the interest grew feverish, even futuristic. His aunt-and-then-mother-in-law, Maria Clemm, who remained devoted to Poe after Virginia's death, would remember how they sat up together until four in the morning, Poe working, she keeping him company.

"When he was composing 'Eureka,' we used to walk up and down the garden, his arm around me, mine around him, until I was so tired I could not walk," she said. "He would stop every few minutes and explain his ideas to me, and ask if I understood him." Soon, Poe was ready to ask the outside world the same question. He placed an ad in the *Daily Tribune* to make the announcement.

> Edgar A. Poe will lecture at the Society Library on Thursday evening, the 3d inst. At half-past 7. Subject, "The Universe." Tickets 50 cents—to be had at the door.

On the night of February 3, 1848, Poe stepped up to the lectern and began his lecture by reading a letter from the year 2848. Except it was not really a letter from 1,000 years into the future—it was a punning, jokey satire of different types of scientific reasoning. From there, he moved on to reveal our "Universe of Stars" in all its various dimensions and possibilities, expounding on the secrets of space, light, consciousness, and God. The Creator was an author, like himself, Poe explained, and what we take to be our experience is in fact an elaborate plot devised by Him for reasons never understood until Poe himself had divined them. *Poe* had intuited the beginning of the universe—a "primordial particle," a oneness from which everything proceeded—and the end of it, too. Eventually, in an eon or two, our souls as well as God's soul, the stars, and all other matter were going to collapse back into oneness, a glorious "common embrace." Destruction and ruin lay ahead, but ultimately so did renewal.

He kept talking, on and on and on in this vein, for two and a half hours.

You have to imagine the audience squirming in their seats. It must have been all they could do not to cry, "What is this shit?" out loud. "Some of us began to be quite sensible of the lapse of time," a reviewer for the *New World* moaned later, in print. "Still no end was visible; the thin leaves, one after another, of the neat manuscript, were gracefully turned over; yet, oh, a plenty more were evidently left behind, abiding patiently 'their appointed time.'" Even one of Poe's friends described the lecture as a "mountainous piece of absurdity" which "drove people from the room."

Except Poe never knew, or maybe he just didn't care. Some weeks after the lecture, totally undaunted, he marched into the offices of George Palmer Putnam—one of the most powerful publishers in America at that time—and told Putnam that no other scientific event in the history of the world approached in importance the original developments of *Eureka*. By comparison, Isaac Newton's discovery of gravity was a mere footnote. But if Putnam wanted to publish *Eureka*, he had better understand that doing so meant giving up all other publishing activity, without exception. An edition of 50,000 copies might be sufficient to start with, yet it would be only the beginning, because *Eureka* was going to make them both famous and filthily, fiendishly rich. Both of them would be lauded as visionaries, and both of them would realize the magnificent fortunes they'd been seeking vainly their entire careers.

Incredibly, Putnam saw promise in this scheme. He would eventually publish *Eureka*, but in 500 copies rather than 50,000. It sold poorly, though that it sold at all seems remarkable. Some critics now see Poe as having predicted the Big Bang theory and the idea of the multiverse, as well as a host of other, later discoveries. Others describe *Eureka* as a work of "crank literature," such as Poe biographer Paul Collins, viewing

Poe himself—at least during this phase of his life—as a crackpot, a babbling kook in a tinfoil hat, maybe even a bit of a fraud. And it's possible both views are right. Poe might have intuited some advanced scientific facts and theories, and at the same time he may also have been half-mad, operating from a place of deep delusion and manic grandiosity.

You might see in Poe's *Eureka* phase your classic meltdown: the 1848 equivalent of Van Gogh chopping off his ear before hand-delivering it to a brothel maid, or Britney Spears first shaving her head, then attacking a minivan with an umbrella, only shaped by Poe's obsessive nature and unique genius. In this light, you almost *have to* admire his originality, his risk-taking—the unapologetic, grief-induced, galaxy-brained leap he made.* Was there any better way for him to process the death of someone he loved so much? Maybe, but probably not. And here's the thing: you can avail yourself of the same techniques to process death, or those events of great rupture, like breakups or the final episode of *Mad Men*, that can *feel* like a sort of death.

For some people, the tendency in responding to profound hurt is first to wallow, then to follow some conventional path to self-improvement. You might go from holing up alone in your dank apartment to—weeks or months later—hitting the gym, taking a ceramics class, rebooting your Duolingo account, or rebounding with some new lover (or three) in quick succession. This track roughly follows the traditional stages

---

*"Galaxy brain" to mean the vast assumptions that people sometimes make, especially in cases where their reach exceeds their grasp. Google "galaxy brain meme" for a visual representation or see page 126.

of grief identified by the psychologist Elisabeth Kübler-Ross in the late 1960s: denial, anger, depression, bargaining, and acceptance.*

Kübler-Ross recognized that the bargaining stage often includes the grieving person seeking meaning, pondering the *whys* of what happened. Poe's example suggests this phase may be its own distinct phenomenon, one that we can exploit for ourselves. Life offers us so few pretexts to radically change our own minds and shift our settled habits, that if breakups and death don't give us the space to swerve, what possibly could?

All our lives, we mostly take events and new information as confirmation of what we already think, whereas a profound crisis may guide us toward startling insights, helping us make our own *Eureka*-like intuitive leaps. When you're utterly beaten, abject, humbled, reduced by suffering to your most vulnerable, cracked-open self, that can be the perfect time to tune into emanations from beyond—whether from science, religion, mysticism, art, psychology, tequila, ayahuasca, or some potent combination of all these things. In fact, just a few years before he loosed *Eureka* upon the world, Poe remarked that "all the important good resolutions which we keep—all startling, marked regenerations of character" occur during the most profound "*crises* of life."

This isn't to make fun of breakdowns, or cast intense mental and emotional pain in a rosy light. None of us would ever choose to have our hearts smashed, or be driven to such extremities by depression and/or the horrendous suffering of those we love most. But agony is coming for us all—remember that tolling bell?—and grieving is an inescapable part of life.

---

* Why she left out "write a 40,000-word Theory of Everything" is the subject of another book—just not one by me.

The most you can do is seek meaning, so why not lean into this life phase that sees you parsing cosmic vibrations, grasping after new realizations, swimming into the deep end for the first time in years? Let's look at how you might do just that, following Poe's template.

1. Go big

What *Eureka* allowed Poe to do was work out his loss on a grand scale. Nothing less than the entire universe was brought in to explain his pain and help him understand why human life and love are destined to go to shit. When pain comes for you, you should feel entitled to go just as big. You might abruptly switch careers, convert to a new religion, move to a new country, change your political ideology, or write a questionable 40,000-word scientific and metaphysical treatise/prose poem. The point is, don't waste this once-in-a-lifetime opportunity. Don't diminish your own grief or shame yourself into having a smaller, more modest reaction than you otherwise might. Allow yourself to be shaken to your core.

2. Come up with your own new Theory of Everything

Understood properly, a great big chance lies before you. Seize it and break free from your settled views, arriving somewhere fresh in your thinking and putting your own new spin on X, whatever X may be. What major discoveries will you intuit? What wild ideas will you expound? What magnificent work of "crank literature" will you produce in a yearlong, four a.m. fever, dedicating it, like Poe did, "to those who feel rather than to those who think—to the dreamers and those who put faith in dreams as in the only realities"? Now's your moment.

3. Share your wild conclusions with the world

Make a website, start a Substack, rant on Twitter. Whatever channel you choose, get your thoughts and theories out there. It doesn't matter if you only have ten website visitors or twelve podcast listeners. Almost no one reads *Eureka*, but those who do (including me) often find it to be Poe's most beautiful and fascinating work. Even if you think it's a bit nuts, it sticks to your ribs. The world needs more metaphysical maunderings, not fewer. You may never reach a wide audience, but you will reach a fortunate few of your fellow dreamers—which is plenty enough to hope for and to make the effort worthwhile.

Poe tip #15: If you're going to have a nervous breakdown, go big or go home.

Follow Poe's template and your manifesto may be read decades after your death, at which point you'll be credited, correctly or not, with predicting major scientific discoveries. No matter what, you'll have triumphed. To move toward an expanded view of reality, rather than a reduced one, leaving a record for those who come after you, is the ultimate accomplishment. Nor do you have to wait—complete the exercise below to get started. Then move on to the next lesson in the Poe-gram to learn even more about how to make the work that will survive you (and hopefully everyone else).

Developing Your Own Bad-Yet-Great Case of Galaxy Brain

Using Poe's *Eureka* as inspiration and the galaxy brain diagram as a template, chart your progress from an early inkling of an idea, to a new thought, to a revelation, to a growing conviction, to a full-on, universe-encompassing case of you-know-what.

PART 4
Making Art and Enemies

"I am not ambitious—unless negatively," Poe once told a friend. "I, now and then feel stirred up to excel a fool, merely because I hate to let a fool imagine that he may excel me." But you don't make as big a dent in the universe as he did *just* by undercutting others. Poe was a master strategist as well as a master artist. So let him teach you:

- → Why "flow state" is even better than drugs
- → How to harness your self-destructive tendencies to turbocharge your creative career
- → Why you should troll your peers (and suck up to your heroes)

Plus, peep Poe's #1, only-slightly-sarcastic tip for completing your world-changing masterpiece.

How the Creative Sausage Gets Made

In Poe's 1843 short story "The Tell-Tale Heart," a man is inspired to murder his roommate because he cannot stand the guy's filmy blue wall-eye—can't endure that unseeing yet penetrative gaze.* The murderer's plan is perfect. Patiently, stealthily, he creeps up upon his victim, commits the crime, conceals the body. And then—just as he's about to get away with it, in the very moment that he is chatting away with the police atop the exact stretch of floor under which the victim's body is buried, when all he must do is remain calm and keep a straight face—the man is compelled, irresistibly, to confess.

All while he swears up and down that *he is not mad*. At the same time, he claims that madness has made his perceptions more acute, not less.

> True!—nervous—very, very dreadfully nervous I had been and am; but why *will* you say that I am mad? The disease had sharpened my senses—not destroyed—not dulled them. Above all was the sense of hearing acute. I heard all things in the heaven and in the earth. I heard many things in hell.

---

* And hey, who hasn't been tempted to murder a roommate?

> How, then, am I mad? Hearken! and observe how healthily—
> how calmly I can tell you the whole story.

Insane, or at least half-insane, narrators. Criminal impulses. Mania, melancholia, obsession, horror, despair. The self at war with itself. Poe wrote about extreme mental states again and again, in "The Tell-Tale Heart," in "The Black Cat" and "Loss of Breath," among many others. So it's no wonder Poe the author has been so often conflated with his characters, or that many readers have assumed his themes were personal, reflecting his own dull, dark, singularly dreary mental landscape in the same way that Superfund site of a lake reflects the House of Usher. Few other writers—maybe the Marquis de Sade, Laurence Sterne, or in our own time, Thomas Pynchon—have been so consistently conceived of as a mad genius, labeled as *crazy*.

This is no wonder, either: if you've read this far, you know the conditions of Poe's life meant he worked amidst terrible stress, whether familial, financial, professional, psychosexual, or (most likely) all four at once. And he did admit to being "insane, with long intervals of horrible sanity" during his wife's protracted illness, as well as to alcoholic binges, helpfully clarifying that we ought to understand his insanity caused his drinking, not the other way around. Between this and all the references to opium fumigating his fiction, casual fans could be forgiven for supposing that Poe composed such stories as "The Tell-Tale Heart" while high and drunk.

The whole story of how and why Poe made his art is considerably different. More complex and more promising, too. Assuming Poe's work is his own hysterical confession means trafficking uncritically in the Romantic myth of the tortured artist. More than that, it mistakes the real process by which the creative sausage gets made. It also overlooks the primary psychological benefit that Poe likely realized from his writing—one that is far more reliable and attainable than recognition, fame, and fortune—and one which you too can realize from your own creative efforts, no matter your particular discipline. Or mental-health diagnosis.

It's important to understand, right from the outset, that Poe wasn't just describing his own suffering. His obsession with what we now call mental illness was characteristic of his time. Romantic thinkers, both reacting against previous generations' fixation on reason, order, and rationality, and fascinated by the vicissitudes of existence, the highs and lows of living, wondered if the insane might not have unique insight into the human experience. This dawning sensitivity, as the historian Tim Blanning argued, led to reforms in the treatment of the desperately ill—those lunatics kept chained up in virtual prisons, naked, sometimes whipped and beaten, or gawked at by the public who visited London's Bedlam asylum in the same way they visited zoos. And for some Romantics, their sympathy for the insane rose to something like envy, or positive identification. Weren't crazy people liberated from convention, from all the usual, stifling constraints on thought and behavior? It helped that some of them, Poe not least of all, had had their own experiences of anxiety, depression, and periodic breaks with "reality." What if this made them more gifted artists, not less?

Since the ancient Greeks, madness and genius had been seen as closely allied—Aristotle himself speculated about the connection, as did a host of great thinkers after him, including Shakespeare—and the possible silver lining of this view wasn't lost on the Romantics. Mental illness might help a person access surprising wisdom. It had the potential to earn you extra attention, too—to function as a canny bit of personal branding—and could provide you an excuse for bad behavior if you needed one.

The sociologist George Becker summed it up this way: "The aura of 'mania' endowed the genius with a mystical and inexplicable quality that served to differentiate him from the typical man, the bourgeois, the philistine, and quite importantly, the 'mere' man of talent; it established him as the modern heir of the ancient Greek poet and seer and, like his classical counterpart, enabled him to claim some of the powers and privileges granted to the 'divinely possessed' and 'inspired.'" In short, not only might being crazy (or just half-crazy) confer a kind of special status and help you stand out in a crowded marketplace, it could get you off the hook for shit, too. This ploy remains in wide circulation, as anyone knows who has ever dated a guy in a band.

Poe and his peers were likewise interested in drugs and the altered states drugs could induce. Thomas De Quincey's *Confessions of an English Opium-Eater*, published anonymously in 1821, caused a widespread sensation—and made lazing around and ingesting copious amounts of opium sound like glamorous, sexy fun, no matter the drug's downsides. The great Romantic poet Samuel Taylor Coleridge, an erstwhile friend of De Quincey's who made appearances in the *Confessions*, was also heavily addicted to the stuff. Poe, for his part, seems to have accepted the literary equivalent of a shotgun from these writers. (His own rumored opium addiction turns out to be not much more than smoke and tacky tapestries.)

The Romantic vision of artists as madmen, doped up on their own supply and other substances, helped to give rise to many of the clichés about an artist's life that you and I know today. Somehow, we still buy in to the idea of the mad genius, despite all the counterevidence around us proving that plenty of people suffer horribly, from a wide variety of afflictions, without ever producing a single decent rhyme, much less a poem on par with "The Raven."

That's a shame. And not because the world necessarily needs more rhymes. Creative work, though more than a mere coping mechanism, is one hell of a coping mechanism. It's a way of imposing order on a chaotic universe and of organizing your own disparate, often nonsensical experience. According to twentieth- and twenty-first-century science, sustained dedication to craft results in intense psychological benefits, which means your creative work can bring you more relief, more release than you ever thought possible.

In the 1990s, the Hungarian American psychologist Mihaly Csikszentmihalyi coined the term "flow state" to describe what it's like to feel fully immersed in a task or act of creation, so seamlessly engaged and focused that you're scarcely aware of your own existence. Time passes, unnoticed. The whole muttering, clattering world drops away. For however long you're in flow, you're weightless. You're no longer struggling but experiencing a temporary reprieve from your suffering, a slipping out of the grip of depression, anxiety, unhappy tension. It's a state of alertness and stimulation that doesn't leave you drained or hungover, but, in fact, builds you up. That is why—and I don't say this lightly—flow state is better than drugs.

"Whenever, on account of its vagueness, I am dissatisfied with a conception of the brain, I resort forthwith to the pen, for the purpose of obtaining, through its aid, the necessary form, consequence and precision," Poe said, explicitly describing his artistic process in terms of the relief it provided. Elsewhere he described "that cool exercise of consciousness," "that deep tranquility of self-inspection" through which we glimpse "the most sublime of truths."

Even his (likely borrowed) description of coming out of an opium haze as "the bitter lapse into everyday life—the hideous dropping off of the veil" sounds a lot like someone coming out of flow state back into the real world of dirty dishes, babies crying, dogs whining, your boss calling you, and the rent due. And that's to say almost nothing of the hideous horrors your own head just spins up for you, all on its own, whenever your mental energy isn't effectively channeled.

Flow state is basically what happiness looks like for miserable, self-loathing overachievers like you and me and Poe.* It's what being true to yourself looks like in real time, everything else falling away and your Poe-tential moving through you, light as wind or a yacht-rock melody. Flow state is why artists who struggle to hold down jobs still find themselves able to concentrate, sometimes for eighteen hours out of the day and seven days out of the week, on their *own* work, and don't experience that work as a grind. It's what makes it possible to put in the kind of hours required to get good. To become even competent. To bring your vision to something like life, but better than life.

Poe tip #16: Opium, Adderall, and Prozac are all well and good, but flow state is the ultimate drug.

Of course, not every hour you spend making your art will be like this. Hahahaha, dear God no. You won't achieve flow state every time you open your laptop and boot up Google Docs or Final Cut or Photoshop

---

* Or, as a friend of mine jokes, "egomaniacs with no self-esteem."

or whatever. But you will often enough that it matters, that your overall life is improved. Master craftsmen experience flow, as do dedicated athletes, even gamers. Accountants understand the world through the discipline and order of accounting. Architects and insurance underwriters delight in doing their "deep work," too—as does any workhorse professional turning out a commercial product for general circulation. Aspiring artists and would-be creative professionals alike can access states of happy absorption, too. It's the way, the why, and the how. The best hours of Edgar Allan Poe's life must have been spent at his desk, scribbling, in flow. I say this without much hard evidence but with total confidence. You don't have to be an artist on his level to know.

Some Poe-sible Rituals
to Get You in a Creative Mood

We've all heard the old saw about lighting a candle, doing a little yoga, or meditating to access your most creative mind. Been there, done that. Why not try the following, too?

1. Make yourself a cup of tea or coffee. Decide to unload your dishwasher, maybe do some laundry. Anything to avoid doing your work.

2. Go outside, onto your fire escape or back deck or front stoop, and take a deep breath. Use it to scream curses at the sky.

3. Call up an ex-lover, preferably one who is now happy and wealthy and successful. Put the phone on speaker but don't say a word.

4. Get out a sheet of paper. On the paper, write down all your debts. Tally them up. Now fold the paper into a square. Now into a smaller square. Now into a smaller square. When you can't make the squares any smaller, don a blindfold. Go and hide the paper from yourself, somewhere in your house, somewhere you will never find it.

LESSON #17
Thriving Through Self-Sabotage

Lest we seem to skip past some *very* real challenges posed by the creative personality, let it be said: there is one "radical, primitive, irreducible" trait which Poe, in his wisdom, specifically warned us about. It's our tendency to self-sabotage, sometimes even to outright self-destruct. In 1845, in "The Imp of the Perverse," Poe wrote:

> We stand upon the brink of a precipice. We peer into the abyss—we grow sick and dizzy. Our first impulse is to shrink from the danger. Unaccountably we remain. By slow degrees our sickness, and dizziness, and horror, become merged in a cloud of unnameable feeling . . . out of this *our* cloud upon the precipice's edge, there grows into palpability, a shape, far more terrible than any genius, or any demon of a tale, and yet it is but a thought, although a fearful one, and one which chills the very marrow of our bones with the fierceness of the delight of its horror. It is merely the idea of what would be our sensations during the sweeping precipitancy of a fall from such a height. And this fall—this rushing annihilation—for the very reason that it involves that one most ghastly and loathsome of all the most ghastly and loathsome images of

death and suffering which have ever presented themselves to
our imagination—for this very cause do we now the most
vividly desire it.

In a few words, Poe has put his finger on the inescapable source for
our youthful (and adult) fascination with death—for doing skateboard
tricks without a helmet, for scaling Everest, for heroin. But that same
urge to tempt destruction shows up in smaller ways, too. Maybe you
don't want to risk your own death today. But you might not mind getting
yourself fired.

We are weirdly, paradoxically drawn to ruining our best chances. Those
things we claim we want most? Even as we say we want them, we work to
prevent ourselves from ever getting them. The impulse to self-sabotage is
so strong, so much a part of you, you might think of it as an ever-present
evil elf. Imps of the perverse are like opinions: everyone's got one, and
they reek.

Poe's knowledge of human perversity was, of course, both firsthand
and extensive as possible. In self-sabotage, like any other field of human
endeavor, there can be only one GOAT. Just months after he published
"The Imp of the Perverse," his own imp tempted him into an embarrassing,
highly public spectacle—a self-sabotaging career highlight of sorts.

In what we will call the Boston Lyceum Massacre, in the fall of 1845,
a cohort of powerful tastemakers invited Poe to visit Boston and deliver,
before a distinguished audience, an original poem—with the key word
for Poe in all this being "Boston." Boston was his biological parents' city,
Boston was where he'd tried and failed to make it as a young man, and
Boston was the home of the artistic establishment, a center for the most
revered writers of Poe's age, the literary in-crowd that he both envied and

despised. Giving a talk in *that place* in front of *those people* would give him the ultimate chance to make good. Also, he really needed the money. *The Broadway Journal*, where he was editor and sole proprietor, was already threatening to sink. Booking the gig, he'd pocket $50, or about $1,700 today, plus be honored by his peers as one of their own.

And yet, even as the night of the lecture drew nearer and nearer, Poe refused to prepare. Perhaps his imp was chattering in his ear, holding down his writing hand. He couldn't, or wouldn't, write the required poem.

By the time he stepped up to the podium that October evening, Poe still wasn't ready. So he spent the first fifteen minutes "apologizing" for *not* writing the poem. Such a distinguished audience deserved so much better, he said. He really should've made more of an effort to conform to their tastes. They liked moralistic poems, didn't they? The kind spelling out life lessons so simple any idiot could understand them? His voice dripping with sarcasm, Poe paused, pivoted. Well. The thing was, he *had* written a poem appropriate to the occasion. He began to read from "Al Aaraf," a 422-line epic. "Al Aaraf" is the opposite of a crowd-pleaser. Few people outside academia have ever read it, for good reason. It's all wordiness and pretentious allusions. Poe had composed it some fifteen years before, though he claimed to have written it still earlier, as a kid.*

Audience members began getting up and groping for the exits. Poe kept his head bent over his interminable epic, droning on and on. But his imp didn't let up even after he'd concluded his talk. At a reception following the event, he gulped champagne and kept ribbing his bewildered hosts;

---

* Another instructive example, per Lesson #4 (see page 25), of Poe exaggerating his teenage accomplishments. Remember: Embellish your achievements. Aggrandize your past.

and to *really* stamp down the bad impression, once he got back to his editor's desk in New York, he started publishing articles that drew even *more* attention to the incident. This when rumors were already scurrying around that he'd disgraced himself, acting like a drunken nutcase.

His terrible performance had been a hoax, Poe claimed in the articles. He'd whiffed it *on purpose* because he hated Boston, because the city and audience weren't worthy of him. He'd meant to make an awful impression—

meant to, you hear?! It was like a sad tweetstorm. But in the midst of it, Poe hit on the actual truth. Referring to himself in the royal "we," he said, "It would have been very weak in us . . . to put ourselves to the trouble of attempting to please these people. We preferred pleasing ourselves."

When the Bostonians responded in outrage, among them a popular female editor named Cornelia Wells Walter, Poe jabbed again, below the belt. Or hairpiece. "Say no more about it, you little darling," he sneered at Walter, in print. "You are a delightful creature and your heart is in the right place—would to Heaven that we could always say the same thing of your wig!"

Describing the fallout, scholar Katherine Hemple Prown wrote that Poe "not only refused to deny the accusations made against him, but positively reveled in them." He managed to "fuel the controversy by repeatedly insulting Walter, the city of Boston, its writers, and all of its inhabitants."

You have to tip your wig to him. Poe took an occasion that could have gone merely well, and blew it up into something egregious, name-making, not just memorable but indelible. Just imagine if his talk that night went fine, that he never slunk out of town under a cloud of ignominy. What would have been the result if Poe had followed orders, fulfilled his contractual obligation, done the "right" thing? He would've completed his assignment, delivering some hastily composed poem he didn't really believe in, then soberly returned to his hotel room—refraining from raiding the minibar for $12 Snickers and shots of Grey Goose—then like a good boy gone to bed early and gotten a nice, fresh start the next morning, arriving at the station in plenty of time to catch his train back to New York. And there would be no profound and vital life lesson for you and me to discuss now. None.

For generations, critics and biographers have taken the Boston incident at face value, portraying it as a failure, an embarrassment *par excellence.* That's one way of looking at the picture. But Poe, for his part, knew well the upside in our self-sabotaging tendencies, writing in "The Imp of the Perverse" that we may have "positive need of the impulse," that self-sabotage can be "made to further the objects of humanity." How? By steering us in more interesting directions, toward more radical outcomes.

Sure, Poe's imp shipwrecked his best-laid plans again and again. But then he always responded by doing something bigger, grander, arguably worthier. Right after the Boston Lyceum Massacre, Poe leaned even further into trolling his peers and his audiences, setting himself up for even greater success, as you'll see in the next lesson. Just don't miss the lesson here, as it highlights your own way forward. There's more than one way to make it big. When, inevitably, you screw up some chance, some supposedly wonderful opportunity, the *very next thing* you ought to decide is that that opportunity wasn't so wonderful anyway. Move the goalposts, dear one! Recast your "mistake" as a breakthrough. If it's true that crises are in fact the greatest chances we ever get, then you've actually done this thing right, not wrong. Examples might include:

- ➤ Flunking a class
- ➤ Fluffing some key networking opportunity, or botching a meeting with some important person
- ➤ Not getting into the top program in your field
- ➤ Not getting into *any* program in your field

- ← Not landing that one amazing internship or fellowship

- ← Not finishing an assignment, or not following the rules of an assignment

- ← Making a spectacle of yourself instead of taking that boring, expected-of-you victory lap, then insulting some powerful editor's wig

Because maybe you haven't screwed up after all. Maybe you're just taking a U-turn (or a Z-turn?), figuring out another, more innovative way to accomplish your goals. Maybe your imp had an insight, knowing before you did that the program, the format, the genre wasn't right for you to begin with. What if this opportunity wasn't the best and biggest one for *you*?

Likewise, maybe this job, these people, this project aren't worth it—maybe, just maybe, you should stop seeking the approbation of the world and try pleasing yourself instead because it's the better, ultimately more fruitful and productive, *effectively self-serving* policy. Understood properly, our perversity turns out to be an exceedingly important element of life and career planning, a creative instinct in action.

You might think of your imp as your inner rebel, your inner outcast and iconoclast, sitting at the back of the classroom and muttering sarcastically at whatever the teacher says. What if you let that sinister elf plan your life instead for a while? His or her choices and tastes are much less predictable than that of the teacher's pet, the brownnoser. What is doing everything "right" going to get you, anyway? Most likely, it'll see your originality, all your wildest and most outlandish thinking, neutralized by whatever system in which you're trying to score all those brownie points.

By screwing up, you've made yourself free: free to decide that original thing you wanted isn't worth having after all, and to set a bigger, more spectacular goal—to harness the *power* of your perversity.

Poe tip #17: First, make some plans. Then, sabotage them. Then hatch even *bigger* plans.

Besides, your imp only gets stronger the more you deny its existence: The key here is not to reject but to understand your "worst" self, what it has to offer you. Your perverse streak helps you zag, and if you haven't already noticed, it's one of the great keys to humor. It's funny to admit these tendencies in yourself and to observe them in others. So much of reading about Poe's life is thinking: *Oh man, this fuckin' guy.* If you're anything like me, I expect that is a deeply familiar feeling, one you often inspire in yourself. But it's okay. We survive. In fact, we thrive anyway. Sit back and let your imp take the wheel.

Recasting Your Biggest Mistakes
as Your Biggest Breakthroughs

Complete the simple activity below to uncover some of your wisest and most creative personal choices to date.

1. Describe your greatest academic "failure"—the class you flunked the hardest, the experiment that incinerated the lab.

Now recast it as your greatest academic achievement. What was your imp trying to tell you?

2. Describe your greatest professional "failure"—say, the time you puked from the top of the spiral staircase at the office Christmas party.*

Now recast it as your most brilliant career move. What was your imp, etc.?

3. Describe the "worst" decision you ever made—jilting that ex who later became a billionaire, watching all nineteen seasons of that stupid reality show.

Now describe it as the best decision you ever made. How did your imp inspire you?

---

* Not me, I swear, but I know someone who did.

Trolling as a Fine Art

From his earliest days on the *Southern Literary Messenger*, Edgar Allan Poe reviewed books the way Jack Torrance swung an axe.

Take *Norman Leslie*, a novel written by Theodore Sedgewick Fay, a popular associate editor at the *New York Mirror*, which was then one of the most respected publications in the country. Poe didn't give a damn. In his 1835 review, he screamed that Fay's style was "unworthy of a school-boy," the larger novel "full to the brim of absurdities," "gross errors in Grammar," and "egregious sins against common-sense." In a subsequent article, Poe struck again, labeling *Norman Leslie* "the silliest book in the world."

These attacks did not go unanswered. The staff of the *Mirror* swung back, gleefully informing their far-reaching audience that Poe's own work had been turned down by Fay's publisher and sneering at the *Messenger* for "striving to gain notoriety by the loudness of its abuse." Other magazines joined in, too, calling Poe a quack, a jumped-up faux expert who couldn't, were there a gun to his head, produce one good page himself.

This was the exact fight Poe had been seeking, and—more or less—for the reasons his enemies identified. He didn't care how his nasty reviews unnerved his *Messenger* boss, T. W. White. Instead of backing off, he doubled down. Over the next fifteen years of his career, Poe's criticism remained so caustic and hostile that one victim would characterize it as "generally a tissue of coarse personal abuse." Poe leaped between

professional and personal grievances, then back again, not only inveighing against bad writing, but heaping scorn on people whom he envied. Henry Wadsworth Longfellow, another of Poe's victims, observed: "The harshness of his criticisms, I have never attributed to anything but the irritation of a sensitive nature, chafed by some indefinite sense of wrong."

He would know. Poe initiated his "Longfellow War" in 1845, first in the pages of the *Mirror*, and later in the *Broadway Journal*. To hear Poe tell it, Longfellow was a dastardly plagiarist: a plagiarist so devious and prolific that his plagiarisms could hardly be detected, so rife was the plagiarism, so deep did the plagiarism lie. Equally as bad, Longfellow also had a rich wife, *and* what appeared to be a serene family life, *and* a professorship at Harvard. What a jerk! Longfellow, the most popular poet in the country at that time, could afford to be a gentle and generous soul. He declined to engage, telling friends that life is too short for street brawling. So Poe took matters into his own hands. He clapped back at himself, writing fake letters to the editor under the pseudonym "Outis," keeping the war going and *lavishly complimenting his own work under this guise.*[*]

And Poe still wasn't done. In 1846, as a freelancer once again after the *Broadway Journal* had collapsed, he began publishing his critical coup de grâce: a series of articles for a ladies' magazine that amounted to a literary-world burn book à la *Mean Girls*. In "The Literati of New York City," he profiled several dozen of the writers he'd known or just brushed wings with during his high-flying, "Raven"-fame days in Manhattan, not limiting himself to throwing shade on their work, but also repeating gossip and inserting lengthy comments about these writers' height and weight, posture, facial features (the size of their noses, the shapes of their mouths, etc.), education (or, as he said, their appalling lack thereof), family backgrounds, intimate relationships, even his best guess at the current balance of their bank accounts. Incredibly, some of those Poe covered so ruthlessly were friends, former colleagues—in other words, people who might still have done him favors, and this at a time when he

---

[*] Not everyone thinks that Poe wrote those "Outis" letters, but look them up for yourself and see if you don't agree with me: even beyond the suspiciously apt self-compliments, the obsessive pettiness is a dead giveaway.

was about as poor as he'd ever been. When he was unemployed, unwell himself, and when Virginia was desperately sick—in fact, dying.

Such behavior may seem out of bounds, even morally revolting. And it is. Frankly speaking, from this vantage point in history, it's hard to see how Poe's unfiltered criticism was a great use of his time, except to the extent that it brought him notoriety, attracting the nineteenth-century equivalent of clicks and eyeballs. I hate that it's true, and I expect you do, too, yet trolling—the practice of deliberately provoking others in order to elicit an outsized reaction, whether through an 1840s magazine profile or the modern-day internet—*is* a powerful method of personal PR. A veritable dark art.

Just like us, Poe lived in a chaotic, explosive information age, and he faced the same set of problems about how to stand out amidst a constant torrent of content. To use an oversimplified example: Say you want to create a thriving YouTube channel. Helpfully, the means of video production and distribution have now been democratized, making such a path accessible at all. At the same time, you're competing with millions of other people with the same goal. You can't possibly keep track of all the other content being created, while cultural trends and even whole platforms emerge and disappear with terrifying speed.

Producing your videos may take days or weeks. Monetizing those videos and building your audience, however, may take *years*. It doesn't matter if you're a singer-songwriter, an actor, a comedian, a writer, an animator, or trying to establish yourself in any other field. Standing out is a near-impossible task, and you could be forgiven for trying to find ways of gaming the system—of hacking other people's attention spans so you come to public attention, fast.

Two roads diverge before you. On the left is the Tom Hanks High Road, the virtuous route. You can be polite, even-handed, self-effacing, supportive of others, and here to make friends along the journey. Good luck.

On the right, there is the iconoclast's path, which you will walk alone. You can, like Poe, pose like a fearless truth-teller while letting your aggrieved psychology, your envy of those more successful, and your profound unhappiness with yourself and the world hold sway. You can seek the kind of world-leveling vengeance that Poe sought, at the same time taking advantage of the way human brains are wired to home in on threats and negative statements. Even toddlers understand that "bad" attention is still attention.

You can mine this primitive vein by being pissy, antagonistic, combative, impossible to please or placate, always operating in bad faith. If you choose this path, other people may hate you, and they may be right to. What's more, in strictly practical terms, this route is arguably far more crowded today than it was in Poe's era, and even then, Poe's peers could readily recognize and name his method. Exceptional harshness is now just as likely to work against you as *for* you: Users of YouTube, Twitter, and so on have necessarily learned to tune it out, given how overused and overapplied trolling has become.

What if you were to carve out a middle path? Poe's best criticism was more than mere trolling, and Poe himself, despite some terrible tendencies, more than a mere troll. He was also a literary expert, versed in verse, classic literature, and popular forms, and his command of his field was damn near second to none, even if he occasionally cribbed or exaggerated his knowledge. Your task is to become an expert, too. To really stand out—all the more so now as a negative presence—your criticism needs to be on point, your blows must land. You don't want to be a one-trick show pony, shit-posting only, with no original insights to contribute. What would you think of an aspiring filmmaker who's ignorant of film history? An artist who can't discuss her own discipline, who by choice never visits a museum? A writer who thinks reading books is a waste of his precious time? Such attitudes are for hobbyists and posers—not pros. It's crucial to grasp the history of your field as well as the current landscape of what you're trying to do—a badge of honor amounting to an urgent personal responsibility.

That does not mean you must be a slave to fashion, conventional wisdom, and elitist favor-trading, or that you should automatically accept what is popular as what is good. There's nothing wrong with having an oppositional sensibility *if* you also develop mastery of the material and your own models for judging new work.* In this happy case, your iconoclasm is no longer a pose, and your tendency to iconoclastic overstatement may be fun for everyone involved. Think of Kanye West or Nassim Taleb, endlessly beefing and bitching as though their careers depend on it, yet still being wildly entertaining while they're at it, and at the same time advancing the standards by which they want their own work to be judged.† This is *elevated trolling*, trolling as a fine art. Well educated, well executed. Canny. Worthy. Frequently very funny, too.

We might call this middle way The Path of the Pain in the Ass. Trolling for its own sake, when you have no original thoughts or contributions

---

* Anyone can say of a book, movie, album, painting, "That fucking sucks." A great troll knows how to cut to the quick by saying, "There is nothing original in this, it is just derivative of so-and-so's work, only they learned nothing from the original."

† To be clear, I am not referring to West's politics or his comments on vaccines.

yourself, is just a way of being a jerk. Aim to be more of an articulate pain, someone for whom others can feel at least a grudging respect. The game's no fun for anyone without worthy combatants—and *you* will have more fun when you know what you're talking about, too.

Poe tip #18: Develop a grasp of your field's history and cultivate your own keen critical sensibility. In other words, become a giant pain in the ass.

Another benefit: by becoming an expert, you'll know whom to suck up to, which is every bit as crucial as being able to call out your chosen discipline's sacred cows. You want the people you admire to admire *you*, don't you? Poe did, too. Just as he insulted his overly successful, under-talented peers, he craftily cultivated his literary heroes—particularly Charles Dickens and Elizabeth Barrett Browning—sucking up to them privately as well as writing public paeans to their work. In the process, he *turned them into advocates for his own work*. This strategy can work just as well today, for you. It costs you nothing to send a flattering, even fawning, email, while the upside of doing so may be virtually unlimited. Pick up a few tips in the exercise below before you get cracking. My email address is on my website for whenever you're ready.

Three Tips for Writing an Effectively Fawning Fan Email

Ready to reach out to your heroes? Your initial contact must sing—especially if this person is hit up all the time. Adhere to these guidelines to stand out, Poe-like, from the sycophantic, sucking-up pack.

1. Remember, the magic word is "you." And that means the other person, not *you* you. Do not open by talking about yourself. Instead, in your first sentence, keep your prospect in the foreground and yourself in the background: *Your work changed my life. You're someone I really admire. Your career is so inspiring.* Etc. Don't talk much about yourself until at least halfway through the total length of the email.

2. Focus on clear, detailed compliments. Don't simply say, "I love your work." Include no less than two fully developed examples and be sure to articulate *why* you like the work, *why* it has affected you so deeply. And don't just mention the person's best-known stuff. Focus on the deep cuts, too, demonstrating that you really *have* followed their career.

3. Likewise, play the long game. Don't rush in asking for a favor. Instead, look to cultivate a relationship so you can ask for *bigger favors later.*

Congrats! Attracting Haters Means You Have Arrived

In the least surprising development ever, Poe's 1846 "Literati of New York City" series pissed off many of its subjects—some of whom already hated Poe to begin with and who now, following these fresh attacks, hated him even more.

Poe's former friend Thomas Dunn English received an especially vicious portrait. The article began by seeming to praise one English poem, then calling the poem weak and egotistic before smoothly transitioning to a backhanded denunciation of English as a plagiarist (of course) and a virtual illiterate "without the commonest school education."*

No one would blame English if he sought out some remedial schooling, Poe said. With a little help, English might yet learn how to write a sentence. He was, after all, only thirty-five years old.† "I make these remarks in no spirit of unkindness," Poe concluded, breezily lying. "I do not personally know Mr. English." Never mind that, as you'll recall from Lesson #14 (see page 116), just a few months prior Poe had shown up at English's door asking to borrow a gun, and the two ended up in a fistfight that Poe still claimed to have won.

---

* English was, as Poe knew, a prep-schooler and a medical doctor. *Clearly* uneducated.
† English was twenty-seven. Again, as Poe knew.

In provoking English so publicly, Poe picked a formidable foe, because English had the dirt. He'd enjoyed an inside-the-ring seat at the Osgood-Ellet imbroglio, and he well understood how deserved was Poe's reputation as a drunk with tendencies to wild, sometimes-certifiable hijinks. If that weren't enough, English was, like Poe, a *journalist with connections at major newspapers*. A few days after Poe's portrait of him ran, English's rebuttal appeared in the *Evening Mirror*, ripping Poe a new one in the most public way possible: branding him "an abject poltroon" who stayed wasted for as much as a week at a time, who slandered ladies' reputations, whiffed his professional obligations, and frequently passed out in gutters. So, nothing at all damaging. But English did make serious allegations in saying Poe had committed forgery and borrowed $30 from him under false pretenses.

Taking the bait, Poe soon published a rebuttal of his own. When English again responded, Poe announced his plans to sue English and the newspaper that'd published him, handily drawing the *Mirror*'s editor, Hiram Fuller, into the fight, too. Today, anyone can attack anyone on social media and potentially reach a large audience. In Poe's day, platforms were harder to come by, and few had a larger one than Fuller, who was emboldened to run blind items like this one:

> A poor creature . . . called at our office the other day, in a
> condition of sad, wretched imbecility, bearing in his feeble
> body the evidences of evil living, and betraying by his talk,
> such radical obliquity of sense, that every spark of harsh
> feeling towards him was extinguished, and we could not even
> entertain a feeling of contempt for one who was evidently

> committing a suicide upon his body, as he had already done upon his character. Unhappy man! He was accompanied by an aged female relative, who was going a weary round in the hot streets, following his steps to prevent his indulging in a love of drink; but he had eluded her watchful eye by some means, and was already far gone in a state of inebriation.

Fuller also published a serialized novel English had written, featuring a character named Marmaduke Hammerhead—a thinly disguised version of Poe that allowed English to repeat his claims that Poe was an insane drunk and literary obsessive, a maniacal would-be score-settler, not a man to be taken seriously but someone who belonged in the deepest reaches of an asylum. Wherever, that is, they mothballed the incurable cases.

Despite this onslaught, Poe got the last word. Disheartened yet inspired by the fight, Poe wrote "The Cask of Amontillado," his great revenge tale in which, you'll recall, a certain basement looms large. It's a simple story at first glance. Montresor nurses a secret grudge against his one-time friend Fortunato, so he lures Fortunato down to his family's catacombs-slash-wine cellar and traps him there to die. To get proper revenge, Montresor informs us, one must punish with impunity—never allowing the act of revenge to redound upon oneself—while at the same time making sure one's victim knows *exactly* who has done them down. His long-meditated revenge goes off without a hitch, just the vain rattling of Fortunato's chains.

Only in fiction is such perfect crime possible, however. Real life is messier, plus forensics have come a long way since Montresor's day and age. You and I cannot just go around bricking up our frenemies—too few of us have access to wine cellars, or any training in masonry. Still, Poe's playbook offers us ideas for what we might do when we find ourselves insulted like Montresor, *or* merely in some perverse pique like Poe, unable to stop ourselves from startin' something.

- ➤ If you're going to pick a professional fight, go for broke—pick the most devastating, potentially damaging one possible. Don't attack a rando. Select someone who's seen you at your worst and will have no scruples about exaggerating your flaws.

- ➤ Use the resulting feud as a source of fresh, fiendish inspiration, forcing yourself to succeed at a moment you might otherwise be wallowing in exhaustion, self-pity, burnout, or despair.

- ➤ So long as you confine your score-settling and revenge-seeking to your art, you may produce lasting work that speaks to millions, not to mention avoid a lengthy prison sentence *and* becoming the subject of some true-crime podcast.

Of course, it would be better to avoid this kind of behavior altogether, to never make frenemies, enemies, or rivals to begin with. But given Poe's kind of personality, and ours, it's probably inevitable. Like Mom said, you're not going to be everyone's cup of amontillado. Who says you can't prosper anyway? Sure, mentorships and supportive friendships are important to your long-term creative success. But just as important are those people who make us feel terrible about ourselves, who make us feel like losers or worse—who trigger us to suck in our gut and work harder. So even if right now you don't have any old friends against whom you're plotting terrible revenge, you may want to go out and find some.

One handy proxy is the notion of an online nemesis, popularized in recent years by writer Roxane Gay. Though she never names her nemesis, Gay tracks the person's movements and uses her own Twitter account to record the feelings this person inspires, noting how their good skin and endless professional success both defeat and inspire her. You can do the same. Simply train your eyes on someone in your field who's as successful or—even better—more successful than you are. The result is a kind of frantic focus on what you want and how you're going to get it. As a specific, actionable, and accessible means of channeling insecurity into accomplishment, it's hard to beat.

Bear in mind that your nemesis doesn't have to be aware of *your* existence—the two of you need not be personally acquainted. Your nemesis could be some giant in your field whom you see constantly feted and whom you think is wildly overrated. They could just as easily be a former schoolmate, neighbor, or friend who now has (according to you) the world's most obnoxious Instagram presence. Either can work, so long as your nemesis is able to, in the words of culture reporter Taylor Lorenz, "drive you mad with their achievements." Whatever you're trying to do, the formula is the same.

If you're feeling stuck, feeling behind, find a professional nemesis who ignites your sense of envy and grievance. Now let yourself obsess, let yourself stew. Track the person's career and prepare to race them, the same way you would if there was some showoff revving his Prius right next to you. And consider using envy, jealousy, and/or revenge as more literal themes in your marketing, communications, and creative work. Like the enduring popularity of "The Cask of Amontillado" shows us, such themes are sticky, universal, ageless. Sitting there in English class, teenagers may bristle at having to pick past Poe's archaic language to get to the meat of the story, but all of them understand what it is to crave revenge. Nearly two hundred years since the story's publication, the tangy smack of comeuppance still whets the palate—and, lest we forget, moves merch.

A still more advanced and useful technique involves *using your haters to draw attention to yourself and your work*, and again, Poe shows us the way. During the same period that Poe was tussling with English and Fuller, he may also have renewed his acquaintance with one Rufus W. Griswold, another literary-world peer with whom, over the years, he'd alternately schmoozed and clashed. Griswold had published some literary anthologies that he believed Poe had unfairly criticized. And on one occasion, at least according to a somewhat dubious family friend, Griswold and Poe had dinner together, Poe apparently becoming so drunk that he had to be escorted home to the Bronx by the police. At some point—again, it's not clear when, or even totally clear that it happened at all—Poe and Griswold may also have discussed Griswold becoming Poe's literary executor. Nor is it clear whether Poe ever became aware that *he was, in fact, Griswold's own nemesis*. But this much is certain: he was.

As you'll see in this book's final chapter, after Poe's death, Griswold worked like the most diligent, dedicated (if evil) press agent imaginable, his slanders against Poe drawing an outsized reaction and creating an indelible PR image that wildly exaggerated, and sometimes outright invented, Poe's flaws and crimes. Would Poe have been as successful or closely followed after his death if Griswold had been a decent human being, of sound mind, and if Poe hadn't been his nemesis? It's impossible to know, but frankly, highly doubtful.

Because Poe is always one step ahead of the rest of us, we do have to ask: Was Poe's choice of Griswold as his executor conscious? Could the dignity-mongering, gravitas-craving Poe actually have chosen Griswold as his executor *because* he hoped to be slandered after his death? Given

Poe's deeply perverse instincts and the resulting scandal that Griswold helped create (more on this in Lesson #24; see page 207), you sort of have to credit Poe, once again, with making the most spectacular "wrong" choice possible.

On balance, most likely none of us would choose to be involved in such tussles and battles, but if you are, take heart: frenemies, enemies, and haters may well be the best thing that ever happens to you.

Poe tip #19: Treasure bastards, cherish assholes.
Haters can be even more useful than fans.

Taking an Inventory of Your Enemies

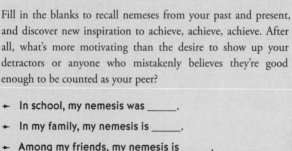

Fill in the blanks to recall nemeses from your past and present, and discover new inspiration to achieve, achieve, achieve. After all, what's more motivating than the desire to show up your detractors or anyone who mistakenly believes they're good enough to be counted as your peer?

- In school, my nemesis was _____.
- In my family, my nemesis is _____.
- Among my friends, my nemesis is _____.
- At work, my nemesis is _____.
- On social media, my nemesis is _____.
- The person I know who isn't aware I hate their guts is _____.
- The greatest enemy I've ever had and sheer biggest bastard I've ever known is _____.

Next, brood on their crimes. Obsess over the ways they've wronged you. Become darkly enraged. Don't worry about it being all in your head—give your hatred and envy free rein. Now suck in your breath and make a damn resolution right now: *In order to show them all, I hereby resolve to _____.*

Composing Your
World-Changing Masterpiece

Every artist craves a formula for composing their ultimate masterwork. It's only natural. And now, finally, you're in luck. Few fans know it, but Edgar Allan Poe left behind explicit advice for changing the world with your art. In 1848, as part of his blog-like "Marginalia" series, he laid out the following instructions.

> If any ambitious man have a fancy to revolutionize, at one effort, the universal world of human thought, human opinion, and human sentiment, the opportunity is his own—the road to immortal renown lies straight, open, and unencumbered before him. All that he has to do is to write and publish a very little book. Its title should be simple—a few plain words—"My Heart Laid Bare."

There's just one catch, Poe said: "this little book must be *true to its title*." Plenty of people would lay their hearts bare if they could, so great is the desire for fame, recognition, and reputation. But a true version is impossible to write. "No man ever will dare write it. No man *could* write it, even if he dared," Poe concluded. "The paper would shrivel and blaze at every touch of the fiery pen."

It's like a recipe where you mix flour, butter, sugar, and eggs, and then at the end, your cake goes off like a grenade. You're all set to reveal yourself in your work, to express your unique truth and let the world in on how weird you really are—except before you can hit "publish" or "upload," your laptop starts to overheat, then to smoke. The screen goes black. Or the crappy little comedy club where you're doing yet another unpaid open-mic night erupts in flames like that climactic scene in *Carrie*, rafters falling on high schoolers.

Is Poe just hoaxing us here, leaving instructions for this doomed task? Why can't we lay our hearts bare—and why couldn't he?

The scholar Jerome McGann speculated that the problem might indeed lie with Poe himself. "Thinking of Poe the man," McGann wrote, "we might surmise that he couldn't face the full truth of his lies, his follies, his plagiarisms, his hypocrisies, all in all, the sum of his failures, which were legion."

But there's a deeper reason, McGann argued. Poe, McGann said, "pushes us to consider that in this impossible quest for truth or fame, one's personal gifts or failings are beside the point." And that's true. No one can take their own measure, whether or not they've spent years embarrassing themselves in public, fudging their age and education, or presenting themselves on Facebook as far more successful and "happily married" (remember Lesson #12?) than they are. Poe knew that we cannot fully face ourselves, and yet there's an even *deeper* issue. No internal *or* external power is holding us back. It's the fact that—because the mission is impossible, because we yearn to accomplish more than we actually can—attempting to do great creative work is necessarily an invitation to catastrophe.

In other words, attempt to make art, and say *hello, please come in* to utter chaos, ruin, and failure. If you've been practicing your craft any length of time, you may be tempted to laugh now in that sudden, painful, gut-clutching way, like you just got shot by the truth. You realize that Poe wasn't simply laying out impossible instructions—he was being brutally honest about what it's like to try.

This is entirely in keeping with Poe's other sly, joking-but-not-really statements about the making of art. As many fans know, Poe had in 1846 written an essay, "The Philosophy of Composition," claiming that he wrote "The Raven" according to an ultra-precise formula—first determining the length of the poem, then the effect he wanted to create, what tone would create that effect, the topic most suited to that tone, and so on, in general claiming that he had proceeded along a strict path of reason and logic to arrive at every element. No drafts, no crossed-out lines. No missteps.

Most *other* writers, he said, produce their work by totally haphazard means involving:

- "elaborate and vacillating crudities of thought"
- "true purposes seized only at the last moment"
- "cautious selections and rejections"
- as well as "painful erasures and interpolations."

Except that's pretty much how Poe composed his stuff, too, no matter what else he claimed or how thick he laid it on about his supposedly methodical process. We know *for sure* that many of the poems and stories in fact followed a formula of draft and revision. Think of "The

Mystery of Marie Rogêt," Poe's 1842 story in which he transposed a real American criminal case, changing the setting from New York to Paris and thinly fictionalizing the real-life story of Manhattan "cigar girl" Mary Rogers, whose body was found floating in the Hudson in 1841. Poe always claimed that he had in fact solved the case—done a better job than the bumbling police and the overheated press—simply by following the clues until he arrived at the solution of the crime. Except that's not how it worked at all. After Poe's initial story was published, it became clear Mary Rogers hadn't been murdered by a sailor, as Poe had alleged in his version. She'd likely died of a botched abortion. When "The Mystery of Marie Rogêt" was published again in 1845, Poe changed the story's ending to make it seem he'd known the real cause of her death all along.

Who can blame him? Many artists, great ones included, make statements about their process, which are, similarly, an ill-mixed cocktail of PR, wish fulfillment, two parts egotism to one part sarcasm. We all wish we had a better formula than the one we're stuck with, invariably some blend of hideous half-starts and retries. Who wants to stumble around in the dark, learning everything too late to get the best out of it, proceeding to a final draft by means of horrifyingly bad iterations that only get less bad *very, very slowly*, through painstaking efforts and many more hours than one would ever, ever wish?* One reason why Poe loved his detective stories and why the rest of us love them, too, is that we all want to be Le Chevalier C. Auguste Dupin: cleverer than everyone around us,

---

* It's not just in making art, either. All of us know the pain of having to live the first drafts of our own lives, making stupid mistakes, rarely getting a redo.

armed with a superior method as well as superior mental ability, floating effortlessly above the fray until coolly arriving at Truth.

If only.

There is our wish for what making art would be like in a better world, and there's what it really is like. An invitation to catastrophe, like Poe hinted: a way of failing, a source of misery and disaster as well as joy. Just look at the portraits of Poe done before he spent twenty years attempting to change the world with literature, then look at the ones taken near the end of his life. You'll see what being an artist can do to a person, the deleterious effects. It's worth asking what did the most damage: the

BEFORE   AFTER

alcohol, poverty, and grief, or writing prose and poetry? Can we separate one set of tendencies from the other?

Probably not. In any case, the illustration is instructive. No matter what your particular pursuit is, or how exactly you plan to make a dent in the universe, you should anticipate horrible pain and horrendous difficulty. Being an artist, as Geoff Dyer once said, means struggling to be an artist. Inherent in this is the notion the struggle will not *end*, either—you won't experience a magical moment of arrival, after which everything gets easier, and the world finally hands you that fat sack of cash and a museum dedicated to the study of your work. But you *can* count on experiencing the downside. Oh yes.

Thinking through the following, therefore, will help you properly calibrate your approach:

Art is work. Adjust your expectations accordingly. Facing the task, you may want to throw a tantrum—to fling yourself to the floor and pound your tiny fists—regressing to an infantile version of yourself when you couldn't have something you wanted, in which immediate gratification eluded you. Fair enough. But instead of hissy-fitting, *settle in*. Change your expectation to "this is going to suck." Your first attempt is going to suck. Your second attempt is going to suck. Your third and fourth attempts are going to suck. Your fifteenth attempt may well suck, too. Nor will you enjoy the work all the time, nor will you remain in a continuous state of flow. You have to keep going anyway. Consider that the far weirder expectation is that the task is going to be easy—or that all that's involved is being honest and raw and bold and amazing, that craft has nothing to do with it. Where did we ever get that idea? Even vomiting is work! Does life in general seem effortless, like some even-keeled, steady state to you? Of course not. Life is hard and mostly awful; there's a lot you'd be justified in bitching about. Once our feet are damp and we're looking around in our twenties, thirties, forties, our expectations should be that existence is and will continue to be enormously difficult. And yet we don't expect hardship, not really. Facing the difficulty, we so-called grownups are as credulous and bewildered as children. That's why we make art, to try and remedy the way that life sucks. Then we run into the awful problem: *Making art is damn near impossible, too.*

Original work is the hardest work of all. The conditions are already challenging enough. But if you're trying to do something even relatively new? Your task just got even harder. It sounds tautological, and yet it's true: things that haven't been done are far harder to do than things that have been done.

Your skills will improve. But that doesn't mean the work gets easier. We can acknowledge that doing our work is not going to be easy, but then our minds slide away like a pat of butter in a skillet. We expect our task will, at least, get easier over time. Eventually, we'll get on the conveyor belt, the motorized walkway. We assume that, after our first success, the second will come more easily. It doesn't. Even the geniuses struggle.

Even the geniuses end up continually revising. Poe, whatever else he said about his process, spent most of his hours with his ass glued to the seat of some dumb, hard chair. He wrote and rewrote, struggling to find time on top of day jobs when he was lucky enough to have those day jobs. Now think of how misunderstood Poe was during his lifetime, *despite these efforts*. He's come in for enormous reevaluation since, and his reputation has grown, but while he was alive, the struggle and sorrow were constant, virtually never-ending. On top of the struggle to compose, there was the struggle to live, and one was not necessarily separable from the other. The same will be true for you.

But here's the rub: if it were easy, everyone would be doing it. Poe's other point in that ironic little injunction about laying your heart bare is that plenty of people would like to enjoy the *rewards* of the work: the recognition, the public life of a successful artist, even the notoriety that can come from self-revelation. What people don't want to do is the work. Which, hey, *is* the saner position. Who can blame them?

Here's the kicker: Poe's idea that creative work is an invitation to endless struggle is not the Romantic view. It's the truth the Romantic myths are meant to conceal. Plenty of artists erase their tracks, feed the myth of their own genius by implying, after the fact, that it all came naturally, no sweat involved. Yet Poe, between the lines, admitted the truth. His art, like most art, comes together from disparate materials—your business sense and your diligence, plus all those wild, conflicting, maladaptive, unstable elements arising from the deepest depths of your soul—even when the end product comes out looking formal and controlled. It ruins your life at the same time it redeems it.

Do anything else if you can. Put this book down right now, go and be free! Ignore the Poe tip, the whole Poe-gram! Forget about laying your heart bare!

Poe tip #20: There's no formula for making great art. Making it is endless work, and the effort might kill you, and it probably still won't be great. If you're extraordinarily diligent and fortunate and capable, it might be regarded as okay. Pretty good. Not bad. Passable, maybe. And then? Everyone will assume it was easy.

Of course, chances are that if you've read this far, you're not actually able to stop, not able to change. In which case, congratulations, you've almost reached the finish line. Being unable to resist your self-defeating impulses is the *precise* qualification you need to move on to the final and most difficult lessons in what Poe called "the iron-clasped volume of Despair." Just turn the page to begin.

Inviting Endless Catastrophe into Your Life

Poe implied that making art was an invitation to destruction—and helpfully, he left behind instructions for following his example. Later, Charles Baudelaire, as if to stamp down the point, tried to write a book called *My Heart Laid Bare*, including a number of strange, even offensive, thoughts and feelings. (Surprise, surprise: Baudelaire couldn't finish the book.) Now's your turn! Finish the statements below and start to lay your heart bare.

Something I have never admitted to *thinking* is _____.

Something I have never admitted to *loving* is _____.

Something I have never admitted to *hating* is _____.

Something I have never admitted to *doing* is _____.

If I could share just one thought or feeling—no matter how personal, weird, inappropriate or absurd—with the entire world, it would be _____.

My grand, heart-baring, unfinishable opus will be _____.

PART 5

The Poe-pose Driven Life: Advanced Techniques

So, self-help has never worked for you, and you've never managed to change your bad habits or improve your outlook so that you see hope and opportunity everywhere you turn. Good job! You're now ready to undertake the trickiest yet *most fundamental* strategies in the Poe-gram. Read on and let Poe show you:

- ✦ Why NOT drinking or taking drugs is a sure path to self-destruction

- ✦ His most appalling moral blind spot—and how to spot your own

- ✦ Why a good pessimism is the best optimism

Plus, peep Poe's tips on how to secure your reputation for decades to come by making mistake after mistake after humiliating, awful mistake.

Personal Growth via Awful, Shocking Vices

Stumbling home from a days-long bender in Washington, DC, in March of 1843, Edgar Allan Poe realized there were a few teeny, *tiny* little items he needed to get off his chest, so he dashed off a letter to two friends he'd seen on his trip. "Thank you a thousand times for your kindness & great forbearance," he told J. E. Dow and Frederick W. Thomas. Perhaps they'd be so kind as to help him out with a few further favors?

- Please don't say a word about how he was wearing his cloak turned inside out, or any other "peccadilloes of that nature," Poe begged. And would Dow apologize to his wife on Poe's behalf? Because he was very sorry "for the vexation I must have occasioned her."

- Also, maybe Dow would, whenever he got a chance, go along to the barber shop above that one tavern and pay the bill "which I believe I owe"?

- Likewise, "Please Forgive me my petulance & don't believe I think all I said."

- Finally, "Please express my regret to Mr Fuller for making such a fool of myself in his house, and say to him (if you think it necessary) that I should not have got half so drunk on his excellent Port wine but for the rummy coffee with which I was forced to wash it down."

It would make for funny reading if these antics had not caused Poe so much embarrassment.*

Poe had set off for Washington with high hopes—and no plans to party. For years, Frederick W. Thomas, his BFF, had been urging him to apply for a cushy government gig. "You stroll to your office a little after nine in the morning leisurely," Thomas explained, speaking from long experience with these kinds of sinecures, "and you stroll from it a little after two in the afternoon homeward to dinner, and return no more that day."

Such jobs, in addition to the part-time hours, paid nearly double what Poe could expect from his crappy editorial positions. In other words, here lay the answer to Poe's prayers. Ensconced within the federal government's generous bosom, he might finally be free—free to write the brilliant work he knew he could write if he could just find the goddamn time, free from money woes. At last, he might discover an escape from drudgery, from despair and the haunting thoughts of what might have been if only he had inherited his foster father's estate. If he'd been as lucky as the less-talented writers he saw dominating the national press, collecting the world's laurels. If, if, if.

Perhaps there was almost *too much* at stake, and this is what made it seem like an okay idea to soothe his nerves with a drink almost as soon as he stepped off the train from Philadelphia. Just the one drink, and no more. Well, maybe a second drink, too. And another and another, until he was reeling around the capital, alarming friends' wives, stiffing barbers, and acting the fool in strange living rooms. Running out of money, too.

---

* Even so, it's still a little bit funny.

But whether Poe drank himself out of a plum position is less clear. Some of the powerful men whom he'd come to town seeking—the ones whom he hoped could hook him up with his dream slack job—weren't at their desks. Thomas himself was sick, laid up in bed, though he evidently observed enough of Poe's behavior to note how Poe "presented himself in Washington certainly not in a way to advance his interests."

Thomas didn't blame or shame his friend. He understood Poe's character too well. "I am inclined to believe, after his sad experience and suffering, if he could have gotten office with a fixed salary, beyond the need of literary labour, that he would have redeemed himself—at least at this time," Thomas wrote later. "The accounts of his derelictions in this respect when I knew him were very much exaggerated. I have seen men who drank bottles of wine to Poe's wine-glasses who yet escaped all imputation of intemperance. His was one of those temperaments whose only safety is in total abstinence. He suffered terribly after any indiscretion." Thomas added that Poe's problem wasn't vice: it was the underlying woe which made the vice necessary.

Being Poe's friend, Thomas was inclined to interpret Poe's faults, failings, and episodes of lampshade-wearing in the best possible light. Yet we might interpret Poe's chugalug tendencies kindly as well, indicating his desperate state of mind much more than rudeness or some appalling lack of self-control. Were Poe alive now, in an age in which pharmacists dispense Wellbutrin and not laudanum, he might make better choices. Maybe in moments of crisis he'd practice yoga, peruse Brené Brown, text his therapist, who knows?

The fact is that Poe lived at a time in which there weren't many healthy outlets for stress; and those who could drink, did, often heavily. Poe's

prime overlapped with the sheer drunkest period in American history. Alcohol consumption in the United States peaked in 1830, with the average person consuming over seven gallons of pure alcohol each year.* By comparison, you and I are teetotalers; today, Americans consume less than a third of that amount. Thus the real wonder is not that Poe drank. It's that he didn't drink *more*. He was always more of a binger, tilting between thirst and ashamed, white-knuckled restraint, than your drunk-every-day kind of guy.

---

* Today, a "standard" US drink contains around fourteen grams of pure alcohol, so this would mean the average American in 1830 was downing what we understand as nearly five and a half drinks per day. No freaking wonder the temperance movement really got going over the next couple of decades, huh? The whole country needed a Dryuary.

Poe did not lack self-awareness about how all that wine, rum, and whiskey affected him, either. He at least had the grace to write his friends an apologetic note, as well as the strength of character to crack a few jokes while at it. He also, just a few months after writing that letter, published "The Black Cat"—his now-famous short story in which a man of gentle instincts succumbs to alcoholism, experiencing a "radical alteration for the worse," growing every day "more moody, more irritable, more regardless of the feelings of others."

In the depths of a binge, the man tortures his beloved cat, and later kills it, soon finding himself haunted by a strange lookalike creature who drives him deeper into darkness, tempting him into even worse behavior. Read the story as an adult, and you'll realize Poe always meant you to know that the man is the monster, not the cat. The horror is in his cruelty, and he is at once both the perpetrator and a victim: He attempts to escape himself, gets drunk, and commits horrible acts. *Then*, to escape the memories of what he's done, he gets drunk again and commits even worse acts. It's a far more complex tale than it seems at first glance—deeply honest about human experience, never mind all the stuff about undead feline tormenters—not to mention a dead-on portrayal of spiraling addiction, a lot like the "drunkalogues" one might hear at an AA meeting.

Unlike successful AA members—tip-top students, Dean's List— however, Poe never managed to quit for good. He kept indulging, climbing onto the wagon only to cartwheel off again, till his final days. Getting too drunk every once in a while might have cost him dearly, but it brought him something, too, he explained. It, too, was about the struggle to glimpse a better, fairer, more beautiful world.

"There are few men of that peculiar sensibility which is at the root of genius, who, in early youth, have not expended much of their mental energy in *living too fast*; and, in later years, comes the unconquerable desire to goad the imagination up to that point which it would have attained in an ordinary, normal, or well-regulated life," Poe wrote in 1845. "The earnest longing for artificial excitement, which, unhappily, has characterized too many eminent men, may thus be regarded as a psychal want, or necessity,—an effort to regain the lost,—a struggle of the soul to assume the position which, under other circumstances, would have been its due."

A quick and dirty translation: literature is the curse of the drinking classes.

The question is, what if our own vices are to some degree necessary, too? Humankind was not meant for voicemail, sexless monogamy, or bosses who "welcome feedback." Our capacities so far exceed such banalities that it's *almost* a joke—and our souls want their damn due, at least every so often. This is not to suggest that you should not get help for an addiction that's ruining your life, but the ones that are passing annoyances and embarrassments? Let 'em be. In our comparatively abstemious age, we often view our more minor failings as clinical, as bugs rather than features of human nature, in need of some cure. But no person is perfect, least of all those Instagrammers who want you to believe they've got all their shit together, that all their faux pas are adorable, and that they never do anything *truly* unseemly once the ring light gets switched off.* Neither is

---

* Show me a person who's got all their shit together, and I'll show you a corpse. Show me a person claiming to have it all together, and I'll show you a grifter asking $2,700 for a weekend "workshop" at an airport Sheraton.

it possible (or desirable, necessarily!) to optimize your way out of every bad habit. The kinder, wiser thing may be to *optimize your bad habits*. Admit them, get what you can out of them, friend. Leave the rest to the angels.

Say you indulge in sex, drugs, and/or whole bags of Cheetos in one sitting. Maybe you can't stop yourself from ranting about politics on Facebook, and now you're in an unwinnable debate with somebody's second cousin while your keyboard is besmeared with cheese dust. The first thing to ask is why you're degrading yourself this way. The second thing to ask yourself is whether you aren't *actively seeking* a little degradation, a little relief from all the balance and rationality that you try to live your life with 99 percent of the time. "Man, being reasonable, must get drunk," wrote Byron. Sure, clarity has its place, but altered states—like the recent fad in experimenting with psilocybin shows—can reveal to us sides of life it's hard to locate otherwise. Spacing out a bit can, paradoxically, bring your world into focus. Besides, how else are you going to reform? One thing overindulging will teach you is to indulge less.

You might be much worse off if you never succumbed to temptation at all and had no shameful habits to give up. Mark Twain pointed out, in his travelogue *Crossing the Equator*, that if you ever want to heal from the illnesses brought on by your vices, you'd better have some vices to begin with. He expressed pity for those unfortunate people who had no option of giving up "swearing, and smoking, and drinking," because they'd never indulged. "These things ought to be attended to while a person is young," Twain advised, "otherwise, when age and disease come, there is nothing effectual to fight them with."

The Russian mystic Rasputin championed a similar idea of Redemption through Sin, meaning that, in order to experience the *maximum* uplift provided by God's forgiveness, it's imperative you first do something that needs serious forgiving, i.e., some form of extreme debauchery. You want to experience God's mercy, don't you? Then attend some orgies first. St. Augustine voiced the same sentiment when he prayed, "Lord, make me chaste—but not yet." Even Ecclesiastes says, "Be not righteous over much; neither make thyself over wise: why shouldst thou destroy thyself?"

Why shouldst thou destroy thyself indeed! Take the Poe tip: Most vices are coping mechanisms that in a better world we would not need. But in *this* world, total abstinence may be as sure a form of self-destruction as its opposite.

Poe tip #21: Sometimes you gotta let your soul assume the position which, under other circumstances, would've been its due.

Recipe for a Peach and Honey

When Poe got his start binge drinking at the University of Virginia, he partook of a certain cocktail called a Peach and Honey. Learn to make your own version, below.

- Moonshine (or, if you don't have any raw mountain alcohol on hand, you might substitute any commercially available peach brandy)
- Water
- Honey or sugar or Stevia, if that's your thing

How to make it

Mix it all together to make a nice, sociable punch with, say, one part moonshine to five parts water, and honey or sugar to taste. Or you can do what Poe did, which was just chug the moonshine, at least according to one of his classmates: "He would always seize the tempting glass, generally unmixed with either sugar or water—in fact, perfectly straight—and without the least apparent pleasure swallow the contents, never pausing until the last drop had passed his lips."

Down the hatch! One glass was all Poe could take, the classmate added, though "this was sufficient to rouse his whole nervous nature into a state of strangest excitement that found vent in a continuous flow of wild, fascinating talk, that irresistibly enchained every listener with syren-like power."

Final steps

Write an apology letter to anyone you've irresistibly enchained with your wild, fascinating talk. Then quit drinking awhile. Maybe forever, maybe not.

Why You Must Question "Reality"

"ASTOUNDING NEWS! BY EXPRESS VIA NORFOLK! THE ATLANTIC CROSSED IN THREE DAYS!" screamed the headline of the New York *Sun* one Saturday in April 1844. "SIGNAL TRIUMPH OF MR. MONCK MASON'S FLYING MACHINE!!!"

Poe, who had arrived in Manhattan a few days before, stood watching as a crowd swarmed the square outside the newspaper's offices—every last person scrambling, struggling, shouting to get their hands on a copy of the special edition. It promised full details of the voyage, "the most stupendous, the most interesting, and the most important undertaking, ever accomplished or even attempted by man."

Mason, the celebrated aeronaut, first attached a wicker basket, or carriage, to the underside of a giant silk balloon. Then, setting off for Paris from the English countryside, he and his crew found their airship in the grip of a gale, bearing them off in the direction not of France but of North America. And so they decided to chance it, to chance everything. With the wind blowing them out to sea and their vessel moving at speed, the vast Atlantic became a "mere lake," a "small pond." They skipped across 3,000 miles of ocean in a sliver of the time it took the era's fastest boat *and* they enjoyed a far better view. At night, leaning over the edge of the basket, the men could look below to see the phosphorescent waters.

"The immense flaming ocean writhes and is tortured uncomplainingly. The mountainous surges suggest the idea of innumerable dumb gigantic fiends struggling in impotent agony," wrote one of the crew in his journal. "In a night such as is this to me, a man lives—lives a whole century of ordinary life—nor would I forego this rapturous delight for that of a whole century of ordinary existence." In just three days' time, the balloon touched gently down in South Carolina, and the same crewman recorded his wonder. "We have crossed the Atlantic—fairly and *easily* crossed it in a balloon! God be praised! Who shall say that anything is impossible hereafter?"

It was the crowning glory of science and technology, the advent of a whole new world. So no wonder that, from sunrise that day until midafternoon, the crush of people outside the *Sun*'s offices teemed so thick that no one could get in or out of the street, while the newsboys could demand almost any price they wanted. At least to hear Poe tell it. "I never witnessed more intense excitement to get possession of a newspaper," he claimed some weeks later, writing about the experience for yet another paper and possibly exaggerating only a tad less than he had in the original story. "I saw a half-dollar given, in one instance, for a single paper, and a shilling was the frequent price." Even he couldn't obtain a copy, he said. Still, to eavesdrop and overhear the comments of readers was "excessively amusing."

Amusing, presumably, because the story was pure bunkum, total bull shit, and the public spectacle of his own devising. Poe had determined to try his luck in New York one more time, and the last thing he wanted was to fail again, as he had back in 1837, his first attempt at the city. Now, here, was *his* signal triumph: a throng of people fighting to get their hands on his words. He'd pulled off the ultimate in guerilla self-marketing, or at least guerilla self-gratification.

That it was all based on a lie made it more enjoyable, not less. No one ever loved a smarty-pants joke more than Poe.[*] Besides, as he said, every detail, every bit of science in the story was accurate, depicting something that theoretically *could* happen. Nor was he wrong. Some seventy-five years after the *Sun* printed that special Saturday edition, a successful balloon journey was made across the Atlantic. And by the 1970s, the

---

[*] Pretty much all Poe's work can be read as satire, not least of all the super-goth stories from "Berenice" to "Morella" to "Ligeia." Poe himself said these stories were "half banter, half satire." One equivalent today might be, oh, I don't know, a self-help book based on his life and work.

Concorde could jet the distance in just four hours, while nowadays you can pull down your complimentary eye mask and drift off to sleep on a redeye from New York to London, waking up on another continent, for a few hundred bucks.

In 1844, however, few people could foresee such a future. You needed a grasp of bleeding-edge engineering, a gift for intelligent speculation, the capacity to imagine a different world. Poe had all this in spades, and he was proud of it. The imagination, he argued in 1845, not long after his "Balloon-Hoax" appeared, ought to be ranked among the "supreme mental faculties" and counted at least as important as reason and logic, capable of bringing man "to the very verge of the *great secrets*." It is by dint of our imaginations, he argued, that we may perceive "the faint perfumes" and "melodies of a happier world." Why should he overinvest in his own time and the supposed realities of *this* world, anyway?* No age which so misjudged and undervalued his talents could be worth taking seriously.

The way we're locked into one measly perspective is the whole problem. According to Poe, our perception is too limited, and our reason so often faulty, that we're *never* seeing the world clearly, *never* grasping reality in full. Professor David Ketterer summed up the point of Poe's numerous hoaxes this way: Poe believed "man exists in a state of total deception," and in devising such jokes, he was "implying that the supposed human condition is also a hoax."

---

* Perhaps you're beginning to sense another theme, too: Poe didn't think this world of ours is so hot. He was always longing for a better one. Justifiably.

Boom! It's enough to blow your mind like a college freshman high for the very first time. And here again, Poe isn't wrong. It's true that our reason is limited, true also that we are all locked into a particular place and moment, unable to see beyond or outside our constraints and get some fuller view of whatever is going on with, you know, existence. You can *try* to pull your head out of your ass, but as any philosophy TA will tell you, it's pretty much an impossible task. Under these conditions, any thinking person is bound to ask the big questions: What is the nature of reality? Of consciousness? Knowledge? Does an objective world exist outside our perception, or is our perception all there is? Is your reality the same as mine? Are we even talking about the same things right now? How long will it be before this overpowerful weed wears off, or should I go to the ER?

Happy people—people who are comfortable in the world and with the world—rarely ask such questions, whereas you and I must live with the tendency. We can't help it. Obviously, if we *could* stop, we would; only the questions occurred to us before we knew to push them away, and now they live forever inside our heads like the chorus from Aqua's "Barbie Girl." Which sucks. But we're stuck: we must wrestle with the most fundamental philosophical questions that humankind has ever attempted to pile-drive or put in the Stone Cold Stunner, so we may as well make the best of it. One perk is—as with being neurotic—you're in the club. You're taking part in a great human enterprise, pondering the issues that history's greatest minds, from Hume to Heidegger, have pondered. Distinguished company.

This points to another advantage. Freed from some silly allegiance to your own place and time, you no longer have to accept your peers' assessment of you and the dissipated, directionless life you're leading, such as it may be. If you acknowledge that your reason is imperfect, it follows that *everyone else's is, too,* so there's no cause to think your brother-in-law is right about anything. As we know, in his day Poe was not particularly well-liked, either—yet now that he's no longer around, begging to borrow twenty bucks, he's beloved the world over. Future critics' judgment of your merits may, by the same token, look very different to what your backstabbing coworkers are saying today. You need not accept your reputation as an unreliable loser or shiftless employee now, trusting that posterity may view you differently, more generously, holding up as your best qualities what are at present taken as your *worst.* In the fullness of time, by people unburdened with the task of dealing with you day to day, your unique genius will be recognized. Surely. No question. The next time you get a shitty performance review at work, simply remind yourself the human condition is a hoax, and *that's* why you're so rude to customers.

Why accept *any* of the settled views and moral judgments of your era? They could be completely, hideously wrong—so grotesque in their inhumanity that posterity clucks its tongue and shakes its head. Trust your hunch instead. Maybe your lifelong simmering problem with everything, your soul's unprompted protest at The Way Things Are, is *entirely justified.* That's a nice, warm, cozy feeling in an otherwise cold world. In fact, it is both healthy and wise to be skeptical of one's own time—most folks who have ever lived have been wrong about almost everything. Question dogmas, challenge limits, and you may just improve your perception, indeed, become prescient. Look at Poe espying the future with his big balloon joke.

Unfortunately, what Poe *missed* is even more striking. You could say it's bizarre that someone who suffered so much, and who wrote so much about suffering, failed to see it occurring right there in front of him, but it is edifying to ponder what geniuses can fail to notice. This is Poe's ultimate anti-example for us, and where the jokes sputter out. For all his prescience, and despite the deep detail of his future visions, Poe missed what we now recognize as the sheer greatest moral problem of his age. We can surmise, from what little he wrote directly on the subject, that he did not object to the enslavement of black people. Worse still, it appears, if anything, that he approved. That his attitude was essentially typical for someone with his background, a white man from the antebellum South, of course excuses nothing.

How could he portray so much horror in his fiction yet not perceive it around him? Because he did witness it. The Allans owned slaves, while the offices of the *Southern Literary Messenger* sat close by Richmond's slave market, which was then one of the largest and busiest in the country, and frankly, if you ever read anything about this market, you will end up kinda glad that in 1865 a massive fire ravaged the city. Poe's moral failure is worth thinking about not because we should get a rush out of feeling superior to him—talk about setting the bar too low—but because the chances are good that, at this very moment, we're overlooking tremendous moral problems in our own communities. Think about it: What will history judge us for? What are you and I missing that's so plain, so huge, we don't even see it?

Poe tip #22: Ask the big questions. In fact, try to ask
all of the big questions.

What Will They Judge Us For?

◄─────────────●─────────────►

What do you reckon is the single greatest moral failing of our
age, the issue that will cause your great-great-grandkids to gasp
and reel, aghast? Could it be the popularity of Justin Bieber? Or
how self-help authors sometimes just stop all the action to start
moralizing? Or, I don't know, maybe something more serious?
Come up with your own answer now.

The Case for Relentless Pessimism

The mummy, once unwrapped and revived with a slight voltaic zap, was happy to chat. He hailed from 5,000 years ago, and his name, inscribed on his sarcophagus, was Count Allamistakeo.

The amazed scientists crowded around, pulling up chairs and pressing their eager questions on him. Wasn't the Count excited to be awoken in this glittering, enlightened future? Just wait until he heard about all the breathtaking developments in science, medicine, technology, engineering, government—at what fifty centuries of human ingenuity had wrought! Railroads, modern architecture, democracy . . .

Well, the Count began, blunt to the point of rudeness. *Not exactly.* All these supposed breakthroughs are, in fact, inferior versions to what he and his fellows enjoyed in the distant past. Take democracy. In his time, it had proved just a nasty, short-lived fad.

The scientists rocked back in their chairs, incredulous. Then the realization began to penetrate, sinking into their psyches, gnawing at their confidence. Everything they had celebrated, now, strangely, disappointed them. Their belief in the achievements of their era burst like a giant silk balloon. "The truth is, I am heartily sick of this life and of the nineteenth century in general," the nameless narrator concludes, in yet *another* moment in Poe's fiction in which he seems to be breaking the fourth wall, turning and speaking right to the camera. "I am convinced that every thing is going wrong."

We should, on the one hand, be leery of reading Poe's 1845 short story "Some Words with a Mummy" as portraying his own personal attitudes. On the other hand, c'mon. The guy hardly ever made such direct, succinct statements. Typically, Poe's prose is freighted with endless asides, piled-up clauses, qualifications, doublings back, obscure and sometimes invented references, tautologies, puns, foreign phrases, poems inserted dead in the middle of a story—to the point that he can be hard to read, much less to quote. But there's none of that here. Poe verges on plain speaking. It's like the very *idea* of progress pisses him off.

"Some Words with a Mummy" is often read alongside a personal letter Poe wrote about this same time. "I have no faith in human perfectibility," he told a friend. "I think that human exertion will have no appreciable effect upon humanity. Man is now only more active—not more happy—nor more wise, than he was 6000 years ago." The result, Poe insisted, would never vary. Later, his tone turned even gloomier. "I am full of dark forebodings. *Nothing* cheers or comforts me," he told another friend in 1849, in fact not long before his death. "My life seems wasted—the future looks a dreary blank; but I will struggle on and 'hope against hope.'"

Even the poem "A Dream Within a Dream," first published in March of 1849 and so often quoted now as though it were some milquetoast, throw-pillow sentiment about life's evanescence, turns out to be about defeated, vanished, vanquished hope.

> Take this kiss upon the brow!
> And, in parting from you now,
> Thus much let me avow —
> You are not wrong, who deem
> That my days have been a dream;
> Yet if Hope has flown away
> In a night, or in a day,
> In a vision, or in none,
> Is it therefore the less *gone*?
> *All* that we see or seem
> Is but a dream within a dream.

You can't hold onto anything. All is loss—all is lost. Not exactly a similar statement to *Live Laugh Love*. Maybe this is why Poe never got the self-help guru treatment before. I don't know about you, but I don't walk away from reading that feeling empowered to run a 5K, hit up my boss for some overdue raise, or finally say hi to that cute barista.

If Poe felt hopeless, he came by that feeling honestly. It's not a coincidence that the daguerreotypes taken in the last years of his life show a guy who's a bit of a bedraggled mess, then a *total* disheveled wreck, a human tear-down. Despite his relative success with "The Raven"—all the fame and praise, very little of the cash—his wife was still sick, and the situation could only end one way. *Did* end only one way. He couldn't hang on to the *Broadway Journal*. His magazine dreams never materialized. He'd wanted to spend his life writing poetry, but spent the majority of his hours churning out hack copy. He got older and earned *less* money, while the bottle gained more and more power over him. He never found another great love after Virginia's death, but tripped through a series of disappointments and misunderstandings involving women who were, arguably, even stranger and less fit for romance than he was. No wonder Poe felt bitter, couldn't concentrate on the bright side! As George Graham, Poe's friend and one-time boss, summarized this period:

> It is true that later in life Poe had much of those morbid feelings which a life of poverty and disappointment is so apt to engender in the heart of man—the sense of having been ill-used, misunderstood, and put aside by men of far less ability, and of none, which preys upon the heart and clouds the brain of many a child of song: A consciousness of the inequalities of life, and of the abundant power of mere wealth, allied even to vulgarity, to override all distinctions, and to thrust itself,

> bedaubed with dirt and glittering with tinsel, into the high places of society, and the chief seats of the synagogue; whilst he, a worshipper of the beautiful and true, who listened to the voices of angels, and held delighted companionship with them as the cold throng swept disdainfully by him, was often in danger of being thrust out, houseless, homeless, beggared upon the world, with all his fine feelings strung to a tension of agony. . . .
>
> Of all the miseries which God, or his own vices, inflict upon man, none are so terrible as that of having the strong and willing arm struck down to a child-like inefficiency, while the Heart and Will have the purpose and force of a giant's out-doing.

Maybe this sounds familiar. Maybe you've felt like you, too, can't do what you want to do, what you know you *could* do if your circumstances would just cooperate for once. You may well have your own sense of being ill-used, misunderstood, put aside—and of all that you might accomplish if money weren't an issue (*the* issue), if your health were better, if the world wasn't so hopelessly screwed-up. Most of us know way too much about rejection: romantic rejection, rejection of our creative work. And we all know disappointment: dreams that never work out, horrifying political developments, tragedies both distant and closer to home. You could be forgiven for wondering if any of this shit is worth it, and whether any of it will ever get any better—or should we all just get up and leave, right in the middle of the movie, no matter that we paid twelve bucks for this popcorn?

In some ways, Poe's pessimism couldn't have been more justified. About a decade after his passing, the country imploded, 600,000 people died in the ensuing war, and though the slaves gained their freedom (patchily, over a period of years), the South later moved to oppress African Americans through a different set of laws, a system of de facto slavery called Jim Crow that would remain in place for decades. Some of the abolitionist members of Poe's generation grew disillusioned, seeing the cost of the change they had sought—but had they been able to look into the future, they might've really started trembling.

Consider what lurked ahead: World War I, the Great Depression, World War II, Stalin, Hitler, the Holocaust, the Rape of Nanking, the murder of civil rights campaigners . . . just, you know, to name a few. Any mummy invited to witness such a future would roll right back over in his sarcophagus, muttering to his "rescuers" to leave the damn bandages on. Yet here we are. You, me, the cute barista. So we have to struggle on, to hope against hope, just like Poe said. The question becomes *how*.

Writing half a century after Poe, the philosopher William James argued that optimism wins out over pessimism because it's the only attitude that gives us a shot at making our hopes come true. James didn't say pessimism is stupid or mindless. He knew better than that, like you do. It's all too easy to find sound reasons to doubt, well, *everything*, the whole human enterprise. So while James's optimism could seem facile, in fact it's courageous, a bracing ethos that urges us to keep trying because trying is all there is.

Italian political thinker Antonio Gramsci expressed a similar idea when he advocated for "pessimism of the intellect, optimism of the will," which lies pretty close not just to Poe's own belief but to the way he actually lived. He kept trying, kept picking himself back up, right to the end. Remember that the last journey he took—the one that ended in the Baltimore ditch—was taken in search of backers for his magazine. So, ditch or no, the guy went down swinging. Now remember how his reputation grew after his death, so that right now there's a Poe action figure perched on my desk, and the annual International Poe Festival is getting under way in Baltimore as I write.

It's true our own accomplishments may not be so grandiose as Poe's. But his life, or more accurately his *approach to life*, suggests that with shrewd and continual and determined effort, we can still articulate our deepest truths and realize our own unique Poe-tential. Best of all, we can do so without giving up our natural gloom and perversity, without forgoing a single delicious calorie of despair. And *that* is the kind of cheerful message even chronically depressed, neurotic, hangry people like you and me can swallow, no?

You, too, can strike an unwieldy, wavering (but honest) balance between experience and expectation. You, too, can choose to press on despite the real and awful challenges you face, which only liars and charlatans would diminish or pretend away. Nor does courage mean not complaining, your upper lip always nice and stiff. Remember Lesson #1 (see page 2)? Complain away! Start bitching now and don't ever stop! Nor does courage mean behaving in an admirable way all the time. God no. Just see the next lesson—the final one in the Poe-gram.

Poe tip #23: You don't have to compromise your pessimism in order to be hopeful—which is itself a hopeful message. Press on.

What Makes Your Life Significant?

In his short story "The Domain of Arnheim," Poe laid out four elementary principles for a happy life—what he called "conditions of bliss." They included:

1. "free exercise in the open air"

2. "the love of a woman"

3. "contempt of ambition"

4. "an object of unceasing pursuit"

The last item in the list is the most important, with Poe saying that the more spiritual and elevated your "object of unceasing pursuit," the better. His own object was the creation of beauty through poetry and prose. Whether Poe experienced much bliss is another question, and he certainly wasn't one to practice contempt of ambition, but he did accomplish his goal, leaving behind a body of work that today is beloved around the world.

Now identify your own "object of unceasing pursuit." Remember, it could be anything, from becoming a "professional eSports athlete" to splicing the DNA of a spider and goat so that you can breed a super species of spider-goats. You just need to pursue it with all zeal.

LESSON #24
Achieving Immortal Renown Through Bad Behavior

All the allegations were awful, and some were outright gruesome: Poe hounded his wife into an early grave just so he could write poems about her. He committed outrages against other women—the implication being rape, or at least attempted rape—and he had sex with his own mother-in-law. He'd been possessed by the devil, too. No, he was a literal *demon*.

"Poets, as a tribe, have been rather a worthless, wicked set of people; and certainly Edgar Poe, instead of being an exception, was probably *the* most wicked of all his fraternity," wrote Scottish critic George Gilfillian in 1854, five years after Poe's death. Gilfillian had never met Poe, but he didn't let that keep him from thundering authoritatively about Poe's "rotten" heart and "infamous" conduct.

"He knew not what the terms honour and honourable meant. He had absolutely no virtue or good quality, unless you call remorse a virtue and despair a grace," Gilfillian ranted. "He died, as he had lived, a raving, cursing, self-condemned, conscious cross between the fiend and the genius, believing nothing, hoping nothing, loving nothing, fearing nothing— himself his own God and his own devil—a solitary wretch, who had cut off every bridge that connected him with the earth around and the heavens above."

How's that for a legacy?

It was, of course, Rufus W. Griswold, Poe's number-one frenemy, who got the *J'accuse* ball rolling, setting all this slander in motion. Before Poe's death in October of 1849, Griswold had somehow kept his near-endless spite and envy to himself. Then, as soon as Poe couldn't slap back, Griswold rushed out an obituary so backstabbing it was practically flecked with blood. One hundred years of pile-on followed, with Gilfillian's hysterical harangue just one example. Poe became Exhibit A when people wanted to condemn poets "as a tribe," or lobbied for bans on booze, like: *Just say nevermore to drugs and poetry, kids.* His terrible reputation oozed the world over.

That Poe's actual behavior fell short of the rumors is saying something, because his actions in the last year of his life were not the kind that might bolster public opinion. As you've seen in the last, oh, two hundred pages, Poe had always been somewhat unpredictable, unreliable, and mercurial—now he grew even more so.

The first months of 1849 found him still living in that Bronx cottage with his mother-in-law, Virginia's death now a few years behind them, yet the grief ever present. Poe earned a little money from sporadic freelance contributions (like a whopping $10 for the masterpiece "Annabel Lee," woohoo!), and he courted other women, all of them unavailable in one way or another. Lovelorn, broke, he thought he might take just *one more shot* at launching his own magazine, maybe look up an old girlfriend or two while he was at it, so he set off on a series of trips.

The problem was, he never fared very well when away from home. At one stop, in Philadelphia, he fell into drinking again, getting sick and speaking wildly. His friends worried he'd commit suicide. Still, Poe stumbled on to Richmond, showing up unannounced at his old love Elmira's house (remember her from Lesson #11?), giving a few lectures in front of crowds who'd known him in his youth, and vacillating in the sticky heat between intoxication and sobriety, at points spending days in bed. So the mystery of what was wrong—what precisely was his medical and psychological condition at the time—actually preceded

---

* The academic Stephen Rachman first made this "just say nevermore" joke, which I have borrowed without asking—thanks, Steve.

his being discovered, senseless, wearing someone else's clothes, in that Baltimore ditch.*

After that discovery, almost no fact is reliable, except that Poe was taken to Washington College Hospital, where the doctors and nurses could not ascertain the exact cause of his distress. He lay agitated, twitching and murmuring, finally falling into a coma-like state and dying a few hours later. Or, to quote Arthur Hobson Quinn's beautiful phrasing, "the poet who had seen farthest into the dim region 'out of space, out of time' went on his last journey, alone." We cannot know why. All the theories about Poe's death—whether from DTs, a brain tumor, rabies, poisoning, or his being kidnapped as part of a low-level political scheme—are pretty much just that: theories.

What is not in dispute is how, afterward, the knives came out. Poe had spent his career carving up his peers, and his knowledge of his own superiority in combination with his combative behavior had made him many enemies, known and unknown to him (remember Lessons #17, #18, and #19?). Chief among these was that rat bastard, Griswold. After Poe's death, Maria Clemm accepted Griswold's claim to be Poe's literary executor, and she seems to have hoped to see a few dollars from the bargain. Big mistake, you might say. Huge. After Griswold published that initial hatchet job, and Poe's friends responded in print, rising vigorously to his defense, Griswold upped the ante with a more "official" biography that repeated, even further exaggerated, the same

---

* There's even debate about whether Poe was found lying in the street outside the tavern, or whether he was found inside the tavern itself. Count me in the "ditch school."

charges. When he couldn't find evidence to support his insinuations, he invented it.

Why? Because Griswold was a jealous mofo and a credential-faking sleaze, all ambition and no talent. He couldn't stand Poe because Poe was everything he wasn't. But greatness invariably means being misunderstood, as Poe knew. In 1849, as part of his "Marginalia" series, Poe wrote:

> I have sometimes amused myself by endeavoring to fancy what would be the fate of any individual gifted, or rather accursed, with an intellect *very* far superior to that of his race. Of course, he would be conscious of his superiority; nor could he (if otherwise constituted as man is) help manifesting his consciousness. Thus he would make himself enemies at all points. And since his opinions and speculations would widely differ from those of *all* mankind—that he would be considered a madman, is evident. How horribly painful such a condition! Hell could invent no greater torture than that of being charged with abnormal weakness on account of being abnormally strong.

Once again, Poe wasn't wrong. If you learn nothing else from this book, I hope you take away the idea that intelligence is a curse; that being smart and perceptive and sensitive is, yes, a "horribly painful" condition; that if you don't conform, they're all going to call you crazy;

and lastly, that the reason you've attracted so many enemies is because you're a superior human being.*

For those of us who, from childhood on, have known ourselves to be alone, different, and supposedly difficult, this should come as a relief. Having read this far, you now know it's simply not the case that all your worldly relations need to be peaceful, that everyone you meet must love you, or that your reputation must remain sterling, unmarred by allegations of demonic possession. Far from it. Other people thinking you're some huge screw-up is, in fact, the greatest positive—the sheer most Poe-sitive—qualification for accomplishment, not the opposite. In fact, the best-case scenario may have you so slandered that for hundreds of years after your death, people still speculate about what exactly dragged you under, and are still full of false facts and misrepresentation about your character.

Imagine if one of Poe's actual friends—say, his early mentor John Pendleton Kennedy, or his BFF Frederick W. Thomas, or his kindly, understanding boss George Graham—had written his obituary, presenting a balanced view that failed to intrigue the public, inflame opinion, and create a broiling, rolling, still-ongoing controversy about the true nature of his character. Would you and I be talking about Poe now? No. *Only by being horribly misunderstood and maligned may we truly change the world!* And yet we're raised with the idea that good behavior, professionalism, decorum, and politeness are the ways to get ahead. It's madness. More

---

* I also hope you've figured out by now that whenever Poe spoke about geniuses in this casual, offhand way, he was talking about himself. It's one more inspiring example. We all should develop such a self-serving worldview. First things first, right?

than that, it's irresponsible. Poe shows us that the best way to stand out is instead to live your own weird-ass, occasionally combative truth.

Even knowing this, you may still find being misunderstood to be uncomfortable. Of course you do—all us superior human beings do— but it's inevitable. You think and feel differently, you behave differently, and like Poe said, you're "charged with abnormal weakness on account of being abnormally strong." People are going to think you're at best a nut, at worst a degenerate. The trick you need to pull off is convincing them that you're an absolutely *terrible* person, completely insane, so that you, too, can get famous and spread your influence to the far reaches of the globe, with your work translated into Thai and Romanian—and John Cusack playing your character someday in a lowbrow thriller. Otherwise you're leaving too much to chance. Whoever got famous for meeting expectations, for paying off all their parking tickets, or putting all their recycling in the exact right bins?

Now, you might be thinking: *But I'm not terrible enough. Yeah, I'm the black sheep in my family, and there are more than a handful of people from my past who probably hope to never, ever see my face again. But I'm not exactly Pol Pot or even Bernie Madoff. I guess I just don't have what it takes.*

Stop right there. Quit that self-doubt right now. I have every confidence that you can blow up your life even more so than you already have. Besides, there's a way around this issue. Don't you know any jerks? Anyone who's prepared to read the worst possible motives into the behavior that grows out of your poverty, your sadness, your hatred of your job, your occasional heavy drinking, and/or your casual possession by demons? Anyone who's willing and able to exaggerate your worst qualities because they have their own terrible insecurities but are too ashamed or stubborn to go to therapy? Excellent!

In this case, you don't have to commit all the sins yourself. Remember, even Poe did not do everything he was accused of. Rather, he simply managed to *piss off the right people*, and the same path is open to you. It boils down to a simple, two-step process—the final steps in the unique Poe-gram this book has laid out for you.

1. Identify your enemy: Do you know any ambitious, insecure assholes? Who's the sheer biggest backstabber you know? Start with a shortlist if it helps, then pick one. Fixate on them.

2. Now make this person very angry. Maybe date an ex of theirs that they're still in love with, or even better, outperform them in your mutual profession. Say "clueless" things in front of them. Let *them* know that *you* know you're the superior person. The rest will take care of itself.

As you can see, this is less a call for deliberate bad behavior than it is for you to boldly embrace contrarian attitudes and to champion unusual ideas, no matter how they challenge whatever establishment or existing balance of power. Non-conformism is the sheer most powerful existential strategy—fail in that, and there's nothing for the bastards to talk about. So if you find yourself condemned, cast out, gossiped about, shut out of the highest circles, be *glad*. You're on exactly the right path—what Poe once called "a route obscure and lonely/ haunted by ill angels only."

He would know. Few writers have ever been as thoroughly hated, discredited, and reviled as Edgar Allan Poe. And it's precisely this notoriety that makes him the towering, universally recognized cultural icon that he is today.

My fellow ill angel, you could do a whole lot worse.

Poe tip #24: A terrible reputation outshines a halo—and always will.

Twenty-Five Ways to Roast a Raven

In "I Am the Walrus," John Lennon sang, "You should have seen them kicking Edgar Allan Poe." Below, feast your eyes on a full list of twenty-five of the worst insults ever lobbed at Poe, by everyone from Mark Twain to Harold Bloom to (ugh) Griswold. Seeing all the terrible things that have been said about Poe, and realizing how vastly successful he's been in spite of or even *because of* all this criticism, will make even the gloomiest Poe fan cackle with glee, as I know firsthand.

Mark Twain (writer and humorist)

"To me [Poe's] prose is unreadable—like Jane Austin's [*sic*]. No there is a difference. I could read his prose on salary, but not Jane's."

Kevin Jackson (literary critic)

"One might go so far as to say that Poe is the worst writer ever to have had any claim to greatness."

Allen Tate (poet and critic)

"Poe's serious style at its typical worst makes the reading of more than one story at a sitting an almost insuperable task."

Aldous Huxley (novelist)

"To the most sensitive and high-souled man in the world we should find it hard to forgive, shall we say, the wearing of a diamond ring on every finger. Poe does the equivalent of this in his poetry; we notice the solecism and shudder."

W. B. Yeats (playwright and poet)

"I admire a few lyrics of his extremely and a few pages of his prose, chiefly in his critical essays, which are sometimes profound. The rest of him seems to be vulgar and commonplace."

Edith Wharton (novelist)

"That drunken and demoralized Baltimorean . . ."

T. S. Eliot (poet and critic)

"That Poe had a powerful intellect is undeniable: but it seems to me the intellect of a highly gifted person before puberty."

H. L. Mencken (journalist and critic)

"[Poe was] a genius, and if not of the first rank, then at least near the top of the second—but a foolish, disingenuous and often somewhat trashy man."

Henry James (novelist)

"An enthusiasm for Poe is the mark of a decidedly primitive stage of reflection."

Rufus W. Griswold (literary anthologist and Poe's literary executor)

"Poe exhibits scarcely any virtue in either his life or his writings. Probably there is not another instance in the literature of our language in which so much has been accomplished without a recognition or a manifestation of conscience."

John Frankenstein (artist)

"*You*, drunken mad-dog, EDGAR ALLAN POE —
Is it my fault that I must call you so?
Your works, like you, are born of alcohol;
Horrid monstrosities, distortions all . . ."

Laura Riding (writer and critic)

"A gloomy and sentimental hack."

Yvor Winters (poet and critic)

"This is an art to delight the soul of a servant-girl; it is a matter for astonishment that mature men can be found to take this kind of thing seriously."

Harold Bloom (professor of literature and critic)

"No reader who cares deeply for the best poetry written in English can care greatly for Poe's verse. . . . I can think of no other American writer, down to this moment, at once so inescapable and so dubious."

D.H. Lawrence (novelist)

"Poe tried alcohol, and any drug he could lay his hand on. He also tried any human being he could lay his hands on."

Ralph Waldo Emerson (writer and philosopher)

"The jingle man."

Hiram Fuller (newspaper editor)

"A poor creature . . . in a condition of sad, wretched imbecility, bearing in his feeble body the evidences of evil lying . . ."

William Crary Brownell (literary critic)

"He evinced the singular cleverness of the children of this world . . . his writings lack the elements not only of great, but of real, literature."

Paul Elmer More (literary critic)

"The poet of unripe boys and unsound men."

Owen Dudley Edwards (historian)

"Endless self-indulgence, wallowing in atmosphere, incessant lecturing, ruthless discourse on whatever took the writer's fancy, longueurs, trivialisations, telegraphing of punch-lines, loss of plot in effect, loss of effect in plot. . . . In sum, what Poe lacked above all was a sense of his reader."

Thomas Dunn English (poet and journalist)

"The very incarnation of treachery and falsehood."

Bryan W. Procter (writer and critic)

"Edgar Allan Poe was incontestably one of the most worthless persons of whom we have any record in the world of letters."

Arthur Twining Hadley (president of Yale University)

"Poe wrote like a drunkard and a man who is not accustomed to pay his debts."

George Orwell (novelist and essayist)

"At worst . . . not far from being insane in the literal clinical sense."

W. H. Auden (poet)

"An unmanly sort of man whose love-life seems to have been largely confined to crying in laps . . ."

CODA

Poe Won by Losing and You Can, Too

Okay, so I'm in the hospital—a bit of a scare, actually—and the attending doctor walks in, lab coat and stethoscope, professional demeanor, a little preoccupied and busy as they all seem to be, and he sees the book on my lap, a two-pound doorstopper of a book, and he leans forward all concerned-like, and says, "Edgar Allan Poe." Then there's a pause. He looks at me, really looks at me for the first time. "Wasn't he *evil?*"

"Not evil per se," I say, clapping my mouth shut on the much longer spiel trying to spill out. *He did have some terrible failings*, I want to add.

He also had some really good qualities! He was not the deranged necrophiliac drug addict you've probably heard that he was, and still there is a grain of truth to the worst versions of his life story. He contained multitudes. He was a genius writer who could absolutely fluff a sentence, and though brilliant, he was pompous and at times a faker, a windbag. His life was terribly hard and so, quite understandably, he was aggrieved and disappointed and often spoiling for a fight, and at the same time, almost endlessly hopeful. He would have had every right to dismiss the universe as hostile and stupid and cruel, yet he managed to forge meaning from his suffering. "To be happy at any one point we must have suffered at the same. Never to suffer would have been never to have been blessed," as he put it. And despite endless financial challenges as well as a poverty of time and resources, he dedicated his life to appreciating and creating beauty. Even if you think a final analysis is possible, Poe remains a complex figure, which is entirely appropriate because we all have a number of different sides, and yet there's so much pressure to be just one thing or another, as if such an elaborate concoction as a person would have just one or two qualities, isn't that ridiculous? How can anyone endowed with the normal allotment of sympathy and a modicum of experience of themselves and other people conclude that there's just one way to be in the world, one way to succeed, one way to live a worthy life?

"Not like evil-evil," I finish lamely, as the doctor makes to leave, perhaps sensing his lucky escape. With Poe, I'm always tempted to elaborate (and then some), gripped by the subject, but more than that, wanting in my own way to do him justice.

The health scare that landed me in the hospital—hefty Poe biographies, raggedy piles of research, and all—thankfully turned out to be no big deal. But I was and am afflicted with textbook PD, Poe disease, not to be confused with ED. That is, I am consumed by a desire to rescue Poe from the depredations of Rufus Griswold and all the lies that Griswold helped to set in motion, with the insults inspiring the defenses, so that balanced views are rare, while saint-or-sinner hot takes abound.

Adding to the complexity, it's impossible to pin down all the hard facts of Poe's life, which cry out for fact-checkers who can tell us which are true, which are false, which are mostly true, which are mostly false, and which deserve five Pinocchios, as so many of the things we think we know about Poe surely do. Poe biography, as a field, is in fact so contested that some of the biographies *have their own biographies*, and there's an entire academic discipline known as Poe Studies. He's like a jigsaw puzzle with a third of the pieces missing, which means that, in the end, the picture that emerges necessarily involves your making a judgment: Storm or mountain range? Castle or shipwreck? Success story or dumpster fire—and what if it's *both*?

"The history of criticism of Poe is the history of individuals who have imposed their agendas on the body of Poe's work," wrote Harry Lee Poe, former president of Richmond's Poe Museum and a descendant of one of Poe's cousins. He's right, and you wouldn't say the situation is ideal. Still, what if every additional layer of interpretation creates a kind of continuity—a "retcon" as it's known in the comic-book world and Marvel universe—building out Poe's story so that it becomes ever more capacious and, in this way, communicates a fuller truth about Poe, even about life itself? What if Poe Studies are like that House of Usher, all rickety backstairs and bat-infested chimneys just begging someone to toss a match into them, or throw a gender-reveal party in the dusty old ballroom? No less than Richard Holmes, that tireless chronicler of

Romantic lives, has said that biography is "essentially cumulative." So, of course, is our experience. That is kind of what experience means, right? One thing on top of another, until we croak.

Now, with this book, we might see Poe's life as a dark, perversely funny triumph of the human spirit. I know I do, and you can, too, if you just try hard enough. It could seem like a reductive view, yet I'm convinced the opposite is true. Once you start to see Poe's life as a kind of absurd victory—and all the more a victory for being totally absurd—your view of the whole human enterprise opens up. In the midst of horrific disappointment, hope appears. So does humor. Then you can't unsee them.

Darkness, failure, un-success? Suddenly you realize how they just might turn to the good over time. It's redemptive in a way people used to believe possible but seems to have fallen out of fashion now that we're all too enlightened, too smart for that kind of sentimental BS. Poe said so, once again speaking of himself in the "Marginalia" via an oh-so-casual observation about geniuses.

"It is a common trick with these fellows," he wrote, "when on the point of attaining some long-cherished end, to sink themselves into the deepest possible abyss of seeming despair, for no other purpose than that of increasing the space of success through which they have made up their minds immediately to soar."

And he lived this example, making up his mind, and if not immediately, then eventually, soaring. Is his success repeatable? The better question might be: Would you want to live his life? One of the consolations of Poe's biography is realizing someone else had it worse.

In any case, Poe's success being repeatable or not isn't the point. You don't have to be on his level to find the story of his life informative, edifying, bracing. Ask me how I know. Jokes aside, I'm more convinced than ever that his life functions in the same way that Joseph Campbell said myths function, giving us courage for the trials we face, establishing a hopeful framework through which we can understand our own most trying experiences. Likewise, I'm convinced Poe's poetry and fiction work in the same way Bruno Bettelheim said that fairy tales work for children, imparting a sense that, while existence may present us with all manner of problems and danger, we have it in us to respond to these challenges.

Poe's heroic unacceptingness, his "gigantic volition," have meant he's remained a lively, relevant presence for 170 years and counting, and so can inspire us to rescue some part of ourselves from the grave, to refuse to concede everything to loss, to death. We should strive to preserve some part of ourselves, too: some remnant of art, love, kindness, even pride. Say it with me: *Fuck you, death! Fuck off, grief! Not today, Satan! Nevermore, dire personal problems! And won't you please quit that bust above my chamber door, Jehovah's Witnesses?*

I trust that is the function Poe performs for you, perhaps more consciously now than formerly, and I hope this book has, in its own small way, contributed to your feeling a little bit happier, a little bit more hopeful and self-accepting, and to your living a more fulfilled life, especially since you are going to pass, like all of us, through the Valley of the Shadow of Death whether you damn well like it or not. You could have been reading anything else, yet here we still are, you and me, on this weird journey that is almost over now. Thank you for taking it with me. Poe is famous for horror, but this time around I think it may be the hope that stays with you—or so *I* hope. Remember, being a weirdo and an outcast is no barrier. In fact, it's as likely to *serve* you. You may feel like a loser, but you can win by losing. Poe did.

Simplistic views of personalities and the world don't do us any favors, anyway. And self-help books that don't acknowledge our perverse side can't account for the range and variety of viable living strategies or what we are *really* up against: not just the problems of the world but the irresolvable, ineradicable problems posed by our own selves.

That Poe has never been treated—comically or seriously—as a model for how to live astounds me because even with the patchy, partial record in his life we see so many disparate human tendencies brought into brilliant relief. If we see ourselves—if, in a sense, the puzzle picture forms a mirror—it's because of what a capacious personality Poe really was, embodying so many different truths. In this way, he gives us the chance to see all the different sides of ourselves, and to see them if not in balance then at the very least as parts of a whole, creating a "unity of effect," such as he strived for in his art.

Spending time with Poe increases our capacity to tolerate contradiction—in him and in ourselves, and dear God, how we need this in an age in which the world spins so fast and yet our biases still manage to outpace us. Even the variety of modes and disciplines you can bring to an analysis of Poe points the way for understanding one's self better—demonstrating how insight may come from anywhere, pop culture or philosophy, history or science, and even, against all odds, dense literary criticism. His example encourages us to take a broader and deeper view of the possibilities for discovering wisdom, and I hope this book has shown you that Poe's strategies for living have much to be said for them, no matter the received wisdom that says Poe was his own worst enemy.

No matter his failings, he indisputably "did the work," both in the sense of a life fully lived despite poverty and a string of horrendous disappointments and of somehow finding the energy even amidst the dregs of defeat. Through everything, he kept trying, and the brilliant body of work becomes all the more moving once you understand the circumstances of its creation.

For all the insults lobbed Poe's way, even his harshest critics have been forced to admit his strength. "He had the disposition of a fighter," wrote William Crary Brownell in a 1909 book otherwise keen to tear Poe limb from literary limb. "When his ambitious and sometimes arrogant plans met shipwreck, owing in general no doubt to his own evil genius, he made new ones."

So his personality and personal style weren't to everyone's taste. So his success wasn't—isn't—conventional. It's only appropriate. We are speaking of a triumph of the imagination in a literal sense, of unconventional materials and frankly awful experiences being turned heroically to their best uses. What could be more heartening than to spend time in the company of a man who, despite dire circumstances, strove to touch the face of eternity and *managed* it? As he said himself:

> Look at *me*!—how I labored—how I toiled—how I wrote! Ye Gods, did I *not* write? I knew not the word "ease." By day I adhered to my desk, and at night, a pale student, I consumed the midnight oil . . . bowing my head close to the alabaster page. And, through all, I—*wrote*. Through joy and through sorrow, I—*wrote*. Through hunger and through thirst, I—*wrote*. Through good report and through ill report, I— *wrote*.

> Through sunshine and through moonshine, I—*wrote. What* I
> wrote it is unnecessary to say.

It's unnecessary to say what he wrote because Poe is still popular, still read and reread. Like Baudelaire sensing Poe had articulated his own thoughts, like that distracted doctor dredging up a negative impression from decades before, we are always returning to Poe. Millions of people know Poe as an active presence in their lives—one who inspires them to live bigger, bolder, evil-er.

In the end, he lost everything, including control over his own story. And yet at the same time, he didn't lose it, because he still lurches like a zombie among us, an example of lived Poe-tential and life's Poe-sibilities. Now ask yourself: What are you going to do with your own dark and cruel existence? How will you become the brave, brilliant antihero of your own story? Get out there and seize the night, like Poe.

Carpe noctem.

Final Quiz:
How Poe Are You?

←————————◆————————→

1. When the kids at school look down on you because your biological parents don't have prestigious jobs, do you:

   A) Just ignore them

   B) Try to win them over with kindness and good grace

   C) Resolve to focus on your studies instead

   D) Develop a monstrous ego and, in adulthood, exact revenge on a string of mostly innocent bystanders

2. When your wealthy foster father threatens to cut you off financially if you don't stop insulting him, do you:

   A) Stop insulting him

   B) Tell him that you love him and try to repair the relationship

   C) Attempt to become self-supporting so you don't have to ask him for money anymore

   D) Respond with some threats of your own, plus bonus insults

3. When your inappropriately young cousin expresses some concerns about marrying you, do you:

   A) Stop trying to persuade her to marry you

   B) Look for more appropriate partners

   C) Therapy, so much therapy

   D) Threaten to kill yourself unless she does

4. When your family is at risk of starving and you have no savings, do you:

   A) Get a second job

   B) Try to stick to a budget and look for ways to economize

   C) Nurture your working relationships to ensure steady employment

   D) Get drunk on the job and lose your main source of income

5. When you are giving a lecture to an audience of your peers, do you:

    A) Show up on time

    B) Prepare your remarks in advance

    C) Think at least a little bit about what you might say

    D) Ramble on about something you wrote when you were fourteen, get drunk, and tell your hosts that you despise them

6. When in the deepest pit of your grief over the loss of your beloved spouse, do you:

    A) Join a support group

    B) Journal about it

    C) Light a candle at your church and pray

    D) Enter a delusional state in which you believe you've figured out every secret of the universe

Unless you answered "D" every time, you need to read this book again.

ACKNOWLEDGMENTS

———◆———

Though this book is (obviously) not an academic work or serious biography, it *is* indebted to the scholarship of, among others, Arthur Hobson Quinn, John Ward Ostrom, Terence Whalen, J. Gerald Kennedy, Benjamin F. Fisher, and Jerome McGann. I'm also grateful to the Poe blogger Undine for raising issues in Poe biography and for her careful parsing of sources. Any errors are, of course, mine.

In a more personal sense, this book would not exist without Liz Hall, Alan Crawford, Stephenie Brown, and Ben Morris. Thank you to Ryan Holiday, Brent Underwood, Brian Boyd, Tim Kreider, Jane Friedman, and Christine Ward for helping in the embryonic early stages. And thank you to those friends who read the manuscript and discussed the ideas with me: Nat Baker, Ned Crawford, Paul Elliot, Leah Sneider, and Carl R. Baab (who else could I text about the Wilmot Proviso?).

Father John Baab fielded religious questions, and Luke Baab assisted me with James River research. Thanks also to my parents, Carl and Cathy Baab (see that English major paying off now, sort of?!), my godparents Joe and Maryann Cronin, and all my family. Big thanks as well to David and Tom Gardner and The Motley Fool (a happy exception to Part 2, and that rare thing, a great place to work), to Lydia Kiesling, Adam Boretz and The Millions for publishing the original articles, to my incredible agent Andrea Somberg, my intrepid editor Jordana Hawkins, my book designer Rachel Peckman, and Javier Olivares for the wonderful illustrations.

Finally, to my husband, Chris, and our son, Hollis, who helpfully punched and kicked me through the first draft, but napped on the job, a few feet away, during revisions: You two are the whole world, and you make me feel lucky every day.

REFERENCES

Benjamin F. Fisher, editor. *Poe in His Own Time: A Biographical Chronicle of His Life, Drawn from Recollections, Interviews, and Memoirs by Family, Friends, and Associates.* Iowa City: University of Iowa Press, 2010.

Jerome McGann. *The Poet Edgar Allan Poe: Alien Angel.* Cambridge: Harvard University Press, 2014.

John Ward Ostrom, editor; revised and updated by Burton R. Pollin and Jeffrey A. Savoy. *The Collected Letters of Edgar Allan Poe* (Third Edition). New York: Gordian, 2008.

Arthur Hobson Quinn. *Edgar Allan Poe: A Critical Biography.* Baltimore: Johns Hopkins University Press, 1998.

Patrick F. Quinn, editor. *Edgar Allan Poe: Poetry and Tales.* New York: Library of America, 1984.

Dwight Thomas and David K. Jackson. *The Poe Log: A Documentary Life of Edgar Allan Poe 1809–1849.* Boston: G.K. Hall & Co., 1987.

G. R. Thompson, editor. *Edgar Allan Poe: Essays and Reviews.* New York: Library of America, 1984.

Terence Whalen. *Edgar Allan Poe and the Masses: The Political Economy of Literature in Antebellum America.* Princeton: Princeton University Press, 1999.

ABOUT THE AUTHOR

Catherine Baab-Muguira is a writer and journalist who has contributed to, among others, Slate, Quartz, CNBC and NBC News. A frequent podcast and radio guest, with appearances on NPR and Lifehacker's *Upgrade*, she lives in Richmond, Virginia with her husband and baby son.